MY OPINION

ASIF SARWAR

ISBN 979-888546151-1

Contents

Contents

About Author

I am nobody, I am neither a scholar of Islam nor a degree holder in the field of humanities. I am an engineer pursuing masters from NIT jamshedpur, a curious reader, a public speaker, a student of sociology and Islam, and a critical thinker.

Noam Chomsky, a prominent thinker, once said:

"If anybody thinks they should listen to me because I'm a professor at MIT, that's nonsense. You should decide whether something makes sense by its content, not by the letters after the name of the person who says it."

That's my opinion before you, it's on you to decide.

PREFACE

It's not a book, rather a conversation between you and the author. The analysis is based on personal induction and deduction about specific social issues and religion(Islam). The deductions might be influenced by the author's background and inclinations. It would be unfair to claim unbiasedness. Any piece of writing on social issues is not free from biases. No human can be absolutely unbiased. When we say, we are unbiased, it's the most biased statement against the truth, right and good. In this book, the author has presented a multidimensional approach to put forward distinctive viewpoints on several subject matters and draw conclusions.

These conclusions are not absolute, they are supposed to be organic and can evolve with further researches. To achieve a synthesis of my opinion and yours, the readers are given space to write their conclusions so that, they can test whether they agree with my opinion or not.

It is for those who can dare to ask why? and why not? Some of the chapters will make you uncomfortable by challenging your preconceived notions. One thing is guaranteed, at the end of this conversation, you won't see the society around you with the same lens. You will be critical enough to have a distinct perspective on social issues and stand out in any discourse

If you agree with it, then it is "THE OPINION" if not then it is "MY OPINION". (peace)

PREFACE

It's not a book, rather a conversation between you and the author. The analysis is based on personal induction and deduction about specific social issues and religion(Islam). The deductions might be influenced by the author's background and inclinations. It would be unfair to claim unbiasedness. Any piece of writing on social issues is not free from biases. No human can be absolutely unbiased. [illegible] we say we are unbiased, it's the most bi[illegible] statement against the truth, right and good. In this book the author has presented a multidimensional approach, to put forward distinctive viewpoints on several subject matters and draw conclusions.

These conclusions are not absolute, they are supposed to be [illegible] researcher. To [illegible] readers [illegible]

It's for those who can dare to ask 'why' and 'why not' [illegible] at the end of this conversation, you won't see the society around you with the same lens. You will be critical enough to have a distinct perspective on social issues and stand out in any discourse.

If you agree with it, then it is "THE OPINION" if not then it is "MY OPINION". (peace)

Acknowledgements

Writing a book is harder than I thought, but the presence of these people made it doable.

Sayed Nishat Tanaum, Shubhangi Sahay and Sharique Asdar.

I am grateful for the review and valuable pieces of advice.

I am amazed by the enthralling cover design, thanks to

Jyotsna Roy

And, special thanks to my family and my annoying sister,

Anabiya Fatima, for the creative title.

Pre-requisite

- How to read, think and proceed, firstly detach yourself from any assumption, emotional attachments to any subject and then be exposed to different perspectives.
- In some of the chapters, strong phrases are used. You might come across terms like sexual, prostitute, liberal, conservative, gender, among others.
- The writer is fully aware of the difference between gender and sex, but has chosen to use them interchangeably for the convenience of the general readers.
- If you are simply interested in secular dialect, you can ignore the religious perspectives presented. You will still get a comprehensive understanding of sociological perspectives on a variety of social matters.
- The topics discussed are vast in themselves, necessitating extensive research. Many dimensions can be added to the provided discourse, making it hard to produce a piece of writing that has all of the answers. This book is intended to provide a basic understanding of any subject matter.

PRE-REQUISITE

How to read, think and proceed, firstly detach yourself from any assumption, emotional attachments to any subject and then be exposed to different perspectives.

In some of the chapters strong phrases are used. You might come across words like sexual [illegible] [illegible] conservative, gen[illegible]

The [illegible] is [illegible] between gender and sex but has [illegible] to use them interchangeably for the convenience of the general readers.

[illegible]

[illegible]

[illegible]

[illegible] themselves, necessarily [illegible] extensive [illegible]

[illegible]

[illegible] intended to [illegible] a basic understanding of the subject matter.

I

Men in pink

You must have heard men in black or blue, but not in pink, but why? Many of you have found the title weird. Buffalo is black, Apple is red, but How come pink is related to girls and blues to boys.

If we look at the history, earlier this pink and blue concept wasn't there. In a book called pink and blue written byJo Barraclough Paoletti, it's stated that people always used to treat babies as a baby, not as girls or boys. Gendered dress for a child was after the age of 7, and you might have seen many baby boys wearing girl's clothes and vice versa. Previously, they used to dress their children in white colour clothes. it was because of several reasons like stress on unisex clothing and convenience.

Change in the society was brought by the Businessman and the capitalists after 1960 or 1970, they started manufacturing coloured clothes as a mark for the little child to be identified as girl or boy, the major reason behind the colourization of sexes was not only the identification of boy and girl, but also to increase the demand in the market.

This fetishism and reification of commodities led to these changes in society, and we made them as norms.

"The more you individualize clothing, the more you can sell," Paolett says.

Moreover, even in the early capitalist transition, pink was never the colour for girls.

For example, in 1918, an article published by Earnshaw's Infants' Department said, "The generally accepted rule is pink for the boys, and blue for the girls. The reason is that pink, being a more decisive and stronger colour, is more suitable for the boy, while blue, which is more delicate and daintier, is prettier for the girl".

But this colourization of gender is deeply associated with the capitalist model of the economy, as child accessories are a huge industry. In India, the apparel and footwear industry for kids showed a remarkable growth during 2012-2017, despite recent demonetization. Since children outgrow shoes and clothes very fast, the demand is hardly affected by economic fluctuations, thus decreasing the risk factor for brands and retailers. With the industrialization, and nuclearization of families, the purchasing power of the households has increased. IBIS World listed children's clothing as the safest speciality in the clothing industry, in its 2010 report. This is a prime example, how the economy as a substructure can influence superstructure or social norms. This is where we can say, Karl Marx is still relevant with his idea of economic determinism.

Previously, it was done to identify the gender of the baby, but, I think, when we are older, we are capable enough to show our sexuality by our persona. We generally tend to connect masculinity and femineity with colours. But we already know from the above study, how pink was considered masculine in the past. It's time to eliminate the stigma of the colourization of gender.

Now the question is, Why men should wear pink? Because, it catches attention all around, whenever and wherever you go. When men around you, would dress in the dark, to look more masculine and monotonous, you will command attention with something charming and bright. Your dress would show that you are comfortable with experiments and you are confident enough to stand out and become more powerful, as, in the past, it has been used to represent power. In 1991 pink ribbons were given to New York survival days sponsored by Susan G Foundation. A study commissioned by Cotton USA shows that men who wear pink make 1200 dollars more on an average year (an article by Antonio Centeno, the founder of RMRS). It does not mean that, if you start wearing pink from tomorrow, you would be a millionaire, but this random research highlights a crucial point, that those who are doing well in their field are confident enough to stand out of the crowd. Don't just wear pink because of this inductive superstition, but to affirm your risk-taking behaviour and to reflect confidence. The next reason is that pink goes with most of the colours, pink is a very versatile colour, especially it looks stunning in Asian men with dark complexions.

Nowadays, we are witnessing a change in order, there are increasing trends in women towards dark and strong colours like black, and confident men are pulling it off with brighter colours especially light pink. If not now, then definitely, the future generations would witness the reversal of taste of colour and the norm would go as" Men in pink".

II

Should we replace patriarchy?

We all know, that patriarchy has led to many evils in society, especially against women, it is clear that women are victims of subordination, exploitation, and oppression. The issues of son preference, discrimination against girls (e.g., food distribution, lack of education, freedom, and mobility), dowry, violence against women (e.g., wife-battering, rape), discriminatory personal laws, the use of religion to oppress women, molestation, objectification, prostitution, never-ending unpaid services at home, etc. but men are also not untouched by its harm.

I used etc (etcetera) not because I run out of words, I kept it open, as we are still discovering, what we can consider oppression. For example, marital rape was not a serious crime to the early people, they didn't think of it as oppression, but now we do consider it as a form of dominance.

In this chapter, I will try to understand patriarchy as a social system. In this piece of writing, I would try to bring a comparative analysis on patriarchy, matriarchy, and equality, and present the other side of the coin.

These are the three broad radical ideas of governing a society. Yes, radical, because these ideas in their core are radical to be considered pragmatic, as none of them can be insularly implemented in a fair society.

When we define patriarchy as a social system, in which men hold primary power and predominate the roles of political leadership, moral authority, social privilege, and control of property. it also includes patrilineal, patrilocal features as building blocks.

But, when it comes to matriarchy, it's difficult to define, as we don't have enough substantial shreds of evidence. The existence of a matriarchal society can only be surmised because neither a social anthropologist nor archaeologists uncovered any undisputed matriarchal society. Some people consider any non-patriarchal system to be matriarchal, thus they include gender equality, harmony, peace, non-competitiveness as a part of it, but many academicians exclude them from the strict definition. Today, there are some communities around the world like in mosuo, Khasi tribes, etc, women play somewhat a pivotal role in society and many people extrapolate them as matriarchy, but in actual terms, they are majorly matrilineal or Matrilocal. Many researchers tried to explain how matriarchy would be equal and peaceful setup, but don't you think it's more of characteristics of an egalitarian society. We should not try to synonymously use matriarchy and egalitarianism to justify matriarchy for the future. Do we have any matriarchal society in the duality of patriarchy? we don't have any. Matriarchy is still a highly fantasized hypothetical system, Anything close to this we have, are matrilocal and matrilineal societies, in which women's reproductive roles are highly valued and women are generally associated with domestic work, childcare, and agrarian work.

If there are two elements of society, A and B, and patriarchy is defined when A dominates the system, then by logical order, when B dominates the system, we must call it a matriarchy. This duality exists in the nature of these systems, and we can't change the definition of the system based on a lack of evidence.

So, I would define, Matriarchy as a hypothetical social system where, women hold the primary power and positions in roles of political leadership, moral authority, social privilege, and control of property. We can see how women are in better condition in Matrilocal and matrilineal societies even when they are involved in the upbringing of children and domestic chores. This makes me wonder why there are such disparities in both societies? (explained in chapter 3)

Effects of patriarchy on men

Patriarchy or matriarchy benefits and harass (or would harass) both genders. Men are also not untouched by the dysfunctions of patriarchy. Today, we have a larger number of inmates who are male. Now we can understand this data in various dimensions, as men are physically more aggressive than women, they are the breadwinner of most of the families, the burden on men's shoulders can lead them to adopt illegal ways (dysfunction of the family as an institution)

In statistica, some studies show that men are more likely to get convicted and get greater punishment as compared to women. The degree of punishment can be different for men and women. For example, in our Constitution, the death penalty depends on the nature of the crime whether it's "heinous" or "rare of the rarest". This understanding might differ with the culprit being man or woman, and can further alter the judgement.

Most risky jobs are significantly dominated by men. For example, large participation of men in any army, manual scavenging, powerline installation, a truck driver, etc

Nobody wants to die (except when the integration forces of society are dominant, what we call altruistic behaviour or altruistic sacrifice). Patriarchy tells a man to sacrifice his life for another gender, that might be the reason why in the movie Titanic, jack had to die for Rose to live. Now, we can see some countries recruiting women in the army, but even US and Israel armies don't deploy women in direct infantry combat. Most suicides are committed by men. It might be because of burdened responsibilities, suppressed emotions, and other sociological reasons, which can be a product of a patriarchal social system.

One 2015 study found that for every 1% increase in unemployment, there is a 0.79% increase in the suicide rate, which mostly affects men, they are responsible for the financial needs of at least two or more people in a family.

In almost all countries with some exceptions, a greater proportion of child custody cases go in the favour of women. It burdens women with the fiscal and physical needs of the child which can lead to pauperization (in the UK), but what about the father, Is the father numb to the pain of separation? I am not saying that the custody should go to the father, this norm of custody is based on rational segregation on the needs of a child, as we believe a mother is more important to the childcare.

In all countries, female life expectancy exceeded that of males. This can imply that patriarchy itself, through the sex roles and patterns of behaviour, can be bad for men's health and lead to higher mortality.

A man can't marry without a job even if he wants to, because of the responsibility of being a breadwinner. But a woman can easily marry, she just has to be old enough. If a woman is born in a lower caste family and by virtue of her beauty and feminine qualities* (* subjective), if she marries to higher caste man then her status automatically raises. This can be seen as an avenue of mobility in our societal strata. At least, she will be treated better as compared to the lower caste males. (I used the words upper and lower caste not to attach value or devalue a caste rather, to reflect what's going on in our society). This avenue of mobility is not open for men.

Even today, most women, in general, want to marry a partner of greater height. This is a very small sign of hypergamy, where a woman marries a man of higher status, caste, wealth, lineage, etc. It is rare in our society for a woman of higher status, lineage, caste etc, to marry a man with lower sociological conditions. When we talk about equality in an institution like marriage, it is fairly impossible, because when a relationship began with inequality, then equality can't be a rational expectation. So, the roots of inequalities in our society may beget from hypergamy. If we really want to eliminate inequalities between gender in our society, the first step should be towards a less hypergamous society, which means society should allow a woman of higher caste, status, lineage, or wealth to marry a man with relatively lower or equal social conditions. So, when a relationship starts with comparable statuses, it wouldn't be so easy for one sex to dominate all the spheres of the relationship, although dominance can still be possible. (The above theory has generalized some traits seen prevalent in society, there might be some exceptions.)

The aim of presenting the above data is not to defend patriarchy, but to highlight that a functional social system would always be agathokakological. Any social system or institution has functions and dysfunctions.

Fight against patriarchy

Are we fighting the patriarchy? The answer is no.

Historically, we have been fighting dysfunctions of patriarchy and inequalities created by it, but the dysfunctions have taken different forms. One of the forms is the objectification of women. Many sociologists have undoubtedly agreed that women's dressing has been continuously sexualized. Sociologist Reshma Khan said, there are various prospects for revealing clothing, like socio-cultural, psychological, historical, but sex appeal is a prominent theme in women's fashion.

So, this raises the question, that why women are forced by corporate norms to wear revealing clothes? Why a ring girl should wear a bikini? what if she wants to do the same job in a covered dress, will they allow her to do so? Why do half-naked women in men's wear advertisements? These questions direct me to imply that dysfunctions of patriarchy have not faded, they have taken different forms, and now it's more complex than ever. The danger is, this time, many feminists and women, in general, are complicit in the new forms of patriarchy.

The dilemma is, what if a woman wants to be dressed provocatively, and like to be objectified, then, it comes down to the right of choice, and suffers from liberal moral paralysis*

*(From a liberal perspective, most of the social issues would boil down to the right of consent. On subscribing to this ideology, we have some benefits but losses too. it

is based on the premise of subjective morality, it is very difficult to decide what is too extreme. For example, an individual's consent must be taken before any social relation, whether it's intimacy in marriage or violation of privacy by the government. But it becomes complicated, where we need to balance between the rights of society over the rights of the individual. This is where it becomes ambiguous to apply the harm principle of liberal thoughts to a very extent. For example, right of an individual to be prostitute dilemma, I call it liberal moral paralysis)

Alternatives

To find a more ameliorative system to remove patriarchy, we try to discover a better alternative. Is matriarchy the alternative? Can matriarchy in an absolute form make society better? The theoretical shreds of evidence are not in favour.

When the sociologists say that it's because of unconditional mother's love, matriarchy would be egalitarian, and rational father's love, patriarchy an unequal system. It becomes less conceivable, as there is no substantial evidence for centuries of matriarchal civilizations just like we have in patriarchy. As these are rational speculations based on unconditional mother love, it seems less convincing to me because motherly love is very much limited to blood child relationship, i.e mother would cherish her children more than anybody else and this is not a vice, she had her children for generally nine months and bolsters them for long. This unconditional love would ultimately create inequality between biological and non-biological children. Not all women can take the highest rank of authority, it would eventually cultivate hierarchy. This hierarchy and stratification would be more ascriptive and rigid, based on blood. On the contrary, if a father's love is rational based, then there is a chance of mobility of any gender depending on its merit. Here, I am not attaching value to any of the love as good or bad, rather I'm giving a perspective, how a matriarchal setup can also be equally unequal.

Now some of you might suggest equality as an alternative. I used to believe the same, but when going deeper, I realized that it may not solve our problems. If a woman wants to implement absolute equality, she must be willing to give up her conventional privileges and accept that she will be regarded exactly the same as a man, without any distinction. But, the problem of today's radical feminism is, they want to carry on traditional privileges but don't want to take the responsibilities. Equality consists of equality of opportunity and equality of outcomes. Equality of opportunity is an admirable goal, but equality of outcomes is broadly problematic as it suppresses meritocracy. We can use equality of outcomes to measure inequality to some extent, but it can't be considered pragmatic. Our society needs more capable, competent people in pivotal positions. By comparing the percentage of backward caste or class persons in any social organisation to their proportion of the population, we can measure the extent of inequality. We can also estimate women's participation by assuming they make up half of the population. However, it would be imprudent to fill those positions coercively or aggressively by women or persons from the underprivileged section, instead, we need a robust process to select a more competent candidate among them. Bringing the underprivileged into the mainstream without jeopardising the quality of those recruited is difficult. More privileged candidates are more likely to outperform those who cannot afford basic outlets for better education and personal growth. I am not against reservations, but using equality of outcomes to aggressively match up representation on absolute proportion is impossible, we would never be able to achieve the goal of absolute proportional representation. We might hit an underrepresentation with or without reservation, or an over-representation by aggressively discriminating with the rests.

We claim to ensure equality, yet we are, to a considerable extent, practising equity more than equality. These are two very distinct notions, which is why we have reservations and safeguards in place for socially, educationally, and economically disadvantaged people, including women.

According to the theory of equity, Humans believe that rewards and punishments should be allocated based on the inputs or contributions of recipients and their needs. However, some theorists believe that by proposing a justice judgement model, they can increase the realm of equality. (Leventhal, 1976b). In which, they gave the idea of distributive fairness, which refers to judgments of fair distribution, irrespective of whether the criterion of justice is based on needs, equality, contributions, or a combination of these factors. By needs rule which dictates that persons with greater need should receive a higher outcome or, an equality rule which dictates that everyone should receive similar outcomes regardless of needs or contributions, we would have to compromise on merit, quality, and competence, if we apply any of them in isolation, or we would have to compromise on a representative outcome.

Extremes

There's no denying that there's a thing known as toxic masculinity. It is abstract and imprecise, with no definite definition. It occurs when masculinity irrationally dominates women's micro-liberty. Similarly, we have toxic feminism, which trains women to disown their feminine quality and accept masculinity, while despising the masculinity in men. For example, it's toxic masculinity, when a man objectifies a woman, but it's seen as empowerment when women use their sexuality to climb the hierarchy of power. If objectification is bad, it should always be bad. But eventually, it boils down to the right to choose and stuck in the " right to be prostitute paradox"(liberal moral paralysis). Toxic feminism has given rise to movements like MGTOW (Men Going Their Own Way). It's an anti-feminist movement, for so-called "men's rights." It asserts that males are the ones who suffer as a result of putting women on a pedestal. Men are the ones who are oppressed. Now I would call it an anti-movement to toxic or radical feminism, which advocates for lopsided distribution of resources. The war against inequality and injustice is somehow converted into a war against men, by punishing them for the so-called historical oppression. In history, both the sexes went through persecution by a minority of powerful men. In the name of women empowerment, we have so many anti-men laws but doesn't have a single way to prove a men's innocence.

I am afraid of MGTOW's growing popularity. It's providing a platform for misogynists to insidiously push their agenda. Although post-modernist debates about the existence of masculinity and femineity and their ambiguity in ligation of characteristics. It's also said that controlling your emotions is a part of toxic masculinity. Many men's manly characteristics have been unanimously considered toxic, resulting in an identity crisis. Men are perplexed about how a man should be; they are told not to be overly masculine while also not being a softy; they are expected to be a perfect father and top achiever at the same time, strong enough to protect her girl while also being a gentleman enough to pull the chair for her as etiquette, If you believe the following statement is a misrepresentation of a desirable man, I encourage you to conduct your own investigation and find out for yourself. However, I would say whatever your definition of masculinity and femininity is. If we want roles to have equal value, we must demonstrate that they are equally significant. We should avoid referring to a woman as inferior simply because, she is feminine. Although, significant progress has been made toward gender equality. But gender "equality" frequently translates into the feminine absorbing and adopting masculine qualities rather than having the freedom to express femininity without masculine constraints. We have already lost the race of equal importance in this patriarchal society if we devalue feminine characters by praising masculinity, and no longer cultivating feminine behaviour as valuable, instead just sadistically accept masculine characters to acquire power. On the one hand, there are insensitive dominating society standards that lead to the adverse treatment of women, and on the other hand, there are outrageously unregulated anti-men legislations that are passed in the name of women empowerment. In our efforts to combat patriarchal dysfunctions, we have chosen the extremes to compensate for one injustice by committing another. We have turned to the disempowerment of men in the name of women's empowerment as if that is the only way out. We've turned the process of women's emancipation into a zero-sum game.

The lopsided value orientation on the division of labour is not due to the mere existence of patriarchy, but it becomes contentious when patriarchy is accompanied by capitalism. For example, the Mosuo tribe is matrilineal, matrilocal, and they work in an agrarian economy, so the absence of capitalism has benefited women because the value of work has not become imbalanced between household and outdoor work, whereas in capitalism, women doing the same are considered inferior. If we try to combine matriarchy with capitalism, we will end up getting identical results to what we are seeing with patriarchy and capitalism after hundreds of years. If we flip the order, putting more priority on domestic duties, the disproportionate privilege will naturally move from men to women.

Hierarchy of competence and meritocracy are not evil in a functional society; rather, they are a requirement of the society with fine-tuning of equality of outcome and complete equality of opportunity. As a result, instead of equality and equity, the equality of justice or justice judgement model can be a noble objective. When we examine the concept of equality of justice or the justice judgement model more closely, we can see that there is an attempt to establish a medium ground. The desire for identicality in all aspects of life is based on the erroneous assumption that a man and a woman are identical. We all know that men and women are more alike than distinct. Does this imply that the differences are trivial? Men are more interested in things, whereas women are more interested in people in general. You may argue that this is a social construct, and while I agree that many notions about women's inferiority in capabilities are social constructs, this is not true in many areas, particularly when it comes to temperament and occupation choice. Even in a matrilineal, Matrilocal system, women enjoy their autonomy in the domestic sphere (centre) and men in the outer sphere., Even if technology has made outdoor work more fluid for both the sexes and most of the works previously done by men, "can" also be done by women. But there is a huge difference between "can" and "will".

Why is it so difficult for us to acknowledge that some differences can give rise to different social manifestations of roles for both the sexes? (explained in chapter 3)

We cannot run a society based only on patriarchy or matriarchy or equality. In various ways, the theorists were striving to achieve grand theories of a balance between opposing forces.

An equilibrium of the feminine and masculine, as defined by Friedrich Engels. A merger of the anima and animus, according to Emile Durkheim (Durkheim 1912), the stability of matriarchal and patriarchal positive principles (Fromm 1970); Why haven't these sociologists tried to make this postmodern world matriarchal if matriarchy is so equal and liberating? They were either terrified of women's domination and loss of authority, or they lacked substantial evidence for matriarchy's egalitarianism, therefore they were hesitant to accept a core matriarchy. As a result, they decided to do synthesis. So, what's the solution?

The concept of domination and authority can be broadly seen in two aspects micro and macro. When privilege and authority are seen in the non-individual realm, it's macro, and when dealt with in an individual realm, it's micro. Having this in mind micro matriarchy can exist, and do exist, within this macro patriarchal setup and vice versa, (like in mouso tribes) because we can say that there are areas where there is no absolute patriarchy.

Generally, A mother has a greater influence and power over children than a father (with some exceptions, no doubt). In some cases, women play a major role in influencing the decision of a man, be it as a wife or mother. After the industrial revolution, micro-matriarchy can be one of the reasons for the increasing Nuclearization of the family. The problem arises when patriarchy invades the matriarchal sphere in society or vice versa.

Sociologists are currently working to create a synthesis of patriarchy, matriarchy, and equality. Now, it's debatable to what extent any state can combine these principles and put them into practice for the development of both genders. Men and women have the equal cognitive capacity, but when it comes to domination, men should dominate their realm and women should do the same. In the area of male and female domination, there can be overlap, and that much chaos is normal and functional. Patriarchy, matriarchy, and equality must all work together to balance out and compensate for each other's weaknesses.

Is Islam Patriarchal?

A comparative study would be incredibly significant, regardless of our ideas about patriarchy, but in particular, let's define patriarchy once more: it's a social system in which men dominate roles such as political leadership, moral authority, social privilege, and property control. Its building blocks also include patrilineal and patrilocal characteristics.

It's really difficult to conclude that Islam is absolute patriarchy. Because in order to determine if something is absolute patriarchy or not, it must meet all of the patriarchy's standards. To comprehend Islam, we have a variety of sources. The Holy Quran, authentic Hadith (teachings and actions of Prophet Mohammad (peace be upon him), and Prophet Mohammad's life history are the basic sources. Although the final two sources might be combined and overlap, I like to keep them distinct. The secondary sources are writings and works of scholars, their interpretations, and consensus.

Spiritually, men and women are equal in the eyes of Allah, All human beings will be judged based on their deeds irrespective of gender. we are equal in the eyes of Allah, but we are not relatively the same. It acknowledges the physical, psychological, and sociological differences between the sexes. Our roles and relationships are valued differently.

Why can we argue that Islam has elements of patriarchy? Here, I am not attaching values to patriarchy as good or bad, but considering as a mere social system.

There are several verses in the Quran which has been interpreted in a way that seems to favour men. Before moving to that we must understand whether the favour is honour or responsibility. it is important to make this distinction.

The prerequisites before jumping to the subject-

In Islam, Allah is at the centre of the world and all human actions, whereas in patriarchy, men are at the centre of the world. (I'll try to avoid using the word "God" to refer to our creator because God is masculine, whereas Allah is gender-neutral and beyond genders.).

Quran is the word of Allah, not the own words of prophet Muhammed (peace be upon him). Shariah law is generally understood as the rulings that are derived from the Quran, the teachings of Prophet Mohammed (peace be upon him), and consensus among scholars. There is no book of Shariah like we have our constitution, there is no such book, that's one of the reasons people sometimes take things out of context to justify their action through religion.

Considering the above knowledge, the following are some of the popular examples, where Islam is said to be patriarchal.

In a family, a man is held financially accountable for all of the members. It's a "responsibility," which means a woman is relieved of the financial burden. It is men's job to offer women with stability and support they can count on. One verse implies as Men are maintainers of women because Allah has favoured some over others. Some translate this Ayat as men having authority over women, but this interpretation is not coherent with the spiritual relationship with the creator. People claim this verse to be patriarchal. It is explicit that responsibility is on men's shoulders, but it doesn't mean that men have got authority over women.

Islam tells the women to cover, so it's considered oppression by many people. This process of covering is commonly called hijab in general usage. Even though it's not the word used in the Holy Quran, but we can say that there is a value in the covering of body parts and modest dressing. The interesting thing is before Allah commands the women to cover, Allah commanded the men to lower down their gaze, and when we read more, men are also not allowed to show their body parts. But the extent of covering would differ, which means I am not allowed to wear shorts or go shirtless in public, so modesty in dressing is for both men and women. Secondly, the hijab or niqab is a sign of identity to the believing women, similarly, a beard is also recommended for men. A Muslim man is not allowed to stare at women. Now, having said that, what if a woman or a man refuses to oblige to it, then other people can remind each other with utmost respect and gentleness. But no one can force to oblige because, clearly, this matter is between the person and Allah. We, as Muslims are not allowed to judge other people in any case, because we don't know what is in the heart of the person. A woman, by her choice, wears a hijab or niqab, no one can force it on her. if you still think it's oppression, then why in European countries (most liberal and free society), the number of women choosing hijab to cover is on the rise? There, nobody is oppressing them to cover.

The issue of polygyny. As men are allowed to marry multiple wives but not vice versa. So, when we look at society the Quran was revealed, there was no limit on the number of wives and female slaves. When you read ancient history, you would know how polygyny was a common cultural norm even before the arrival of Prophet Mohammed (peace be upon him). But Islam came to limit it to a maximum of four, followed by strict conditions of being fair and doing justice to all, if you can't do justice marry one (and recommend only one). What could be the solutions, if males were more likely to be killed in wars in the earlier times, leaving behind widows of martyrs? Even now, widows are stigmatised in our society and struggle to meet their children's needs. As a result, polygyny may be the answer, to bring widows into the mainstream. What options would they have had if not for this? Either they had to battle for a job that was already dominated by men, or they were compelled to be a prostitute by circumstance. Various stories have shown how single women refugees are coerced into the prostitute industries, where they are forced to sell their bodies in exchange for food. Marriage is considerably easier in Islam than in any other culture or religion. Because of marital distrust, unmarried mothers in the United Kingdom have been pushed into pauperization. Because they have made marriage so difficult, people find it easy to find a girlfriend or lover to satisfy their desire, and when they get bored with one, they move on to another. Growing individuality, high expectations, apprehension about commitment, and obligations have spawned new forms of partnership, such as live-in relationships. Polygyny is still widespread in our society; we have only just outlawed one kind of polygyny that manifested itself through marriage. In an article published in IFS 2018 by Nicholas H. Wolfinger, I found that the median American woman born in the 1980s has had three sex partners in her lifetime. The median American man has had six partners, but only four if he's a four-year college graduate. Dynamic polygamy is widespread in our society through dating apps. It's conceivable that polygyny can be a solution to some of the problems of our society. Yes, many men have married many women in order to satiate their lust. It's not typical; normally, men should only marry one woman, however, under certain circumstances, it is conceivable to marry multiple women. This is a patriarchal privilege, but it isn't always undesirable. It is a social issue rather than a religious one. In our own country, India, a survey indicated that Muslims are likely to practise polygamy, with 5.7 per cent of the population. Polygamy was found to be 5.8% among Hindus, however other communities, such as Buddhists and Jains, were proportionally more likely to practise it. Tribals were at the top, with 15.25 per cent of them being polygamous. The question is, should we allow polygyny today, the answer is, it depends. In war zone countries where men are more likely to be killed in the war, it should be allowed to protect the interest of women.

But in a country where women are already lesser in number and stigma on marrying a widow has been decreasing, it is not necessary.

Another ruling which can be considered patriarchal is rulings related to divorce (explained in the chapter uniform civil code).

The next issue is with the verses which deal with wife-beating, This verse has been widely misused to justify domestic violence even after knowing that the prophet Mohammed (peace be upon him) had never even slapped anyone (except in war). There was a time, when he was so annoyed with his wives that he left the home for some time but never showed aggression. The verse that deals with it, is talking about a man's fear of his wife cheating on him or if there is a fear of infidelity, the verse lays out the process as the first thing the husband should do is ask her about it, if she still doesn't stop, stop sharing the bed with her, and if she still continues with that act, the last action is in this verse has been interpreted differently by different scholars. The harshest way it can be interpreted as, light beating with a handkerchief and can also be interpreted as to go away from the wife for some days. Snapping with a handkerchief can't be said as violence against women rather, it's a direct manifestation of resentment towards her. Some scholars also interpret it as a symbolic gesture for being upset. There is a clear saying from "Prophet Muhammad (peace be upon him) said, “None hits except the worst amongst you (shirarukum).” -Suyuti, Jami al-Saghir, 1088 and Ibn Sa'd, Tabaqat al-Kubra, 10516.

Some people say it allows a man to beat women, but even in different interpretations of the same word which signifies a range of meanings, there is consensus among scholars that this verse limits the aggression of men towards the women even if she might be cheating. Let's say you are doubtful or you found out your spouse is cheating on you, then you might lose your cool and sometimes, it gets ugly and fatal for the women. As psychologically, men are more aggressive to the things that challenge their potency, and looking at your wife cheating can trigger a nasty reaction from the husband. so, I will leave it to you to think about what would you do if you are afraid your spouse is cheating on you?

The next so-called patriarchal concept in Islam is the rule of inheritance. First of all, there is no mainstream religion that does justice to women by providing absolute property rights to women, except Islam. This is a complex issue of ruling in Shariah, other factors can affect the inheritance but generally, when we talk about inheritance a woman gets half of the property than that of her brother. it seems to be an injustice but it's rather fair. If we make the inheritance equal it would do injustice to the men.

For example, if there are two siblings, one of them is a man and the other a woman, and their father has 150 rupees, the woman will receive 50 rupees and the man will receive 100. Now she can do whatever she wants with that 50, and her brother has no right to use it; nevertheless, the brother must spend his portion of the 100 on her education, food, clothing, and all other expenses. When she marries, her husband will be required to pay her a dowry, known as "meher," which can range to any amount, depending on her wishes. It is her prerogative to set the amount. As a result, she will amass a substantial amount of wealth in the future. if we equalise inheritance, it will be discriminating against men. In that property she would have absolute control, none has the right to take it away, not even her husband, if she wants to buy you ice cream it's a charity or favour from her.

People never study Shariah as a whole, they pick up some verses and rulings, and use them for their benefit. A constitution of any state should be studied in totality, if we pick and choose any provision, it will be an injustice to the soul of the Constitution. Similarly, any rule book should be read with justice and in totality. This rule of inheritance has suffered in the hand of greed, as in our country people take dowry from the bride and we are still struggling with violence against women due to the dowry. Some reports say Women who have contributed a large dowry are treated better than those who have not. If the groom's family isn't satisfied, she could be tortured to death. Unfortunately, Muslim households are not immune to this; the patriarchal idea of man's dominance has led to the acceptance of regulations that are diametrically opposed to Islamic law. The Muslim community has reduced the concept of meher to the point where the bride is never consulted and the groom's family pays "meher" as a pittance, while looting enormous dowries brazenly. Islam made marriage simple by removing the responsibility from the bride's family, but greed has made it harder today.

Similarly, many other issues can be considered patriarchal. I will leave it to you to decide which one is the responsibility and which one is an honour.

Some verses show the non-patriarchal and Matriarchal nature of Islam. when we look at the beginning of the human race and the story of Adam and eve, we know that they ate the forbidden fruit and were sent down to earth. Now they both ate the fruit, but Allah pointed out and highlighted the responsibility of Adam, a man, not eve, a woman. it does not mean that eve didn't do it, but the major responsibility was of Adam.

There are explicitly particular verses in the Quran and teachings of prophet Mohammed (peace be upon him) which signifies that the best among the men are the ones who are best to their wife and family. In one of the narration where

Jabir ibn Abdullah reported: The Messenger of Allah, peace, and blessings be upon him, said, “Whoever has three daughters and he cares for them, he is merciful to them, and he clothes them, then Paradise is certainly required for him.” It was said, “O Messenger of Allah, what if he has only two?” The Prophet said, “Even two.” Some people thought that if they had said to him one, the Prophet would have said even one.

The Prophet Muhammad(PBUH) said, "Your Heaven lies under the feet of your mother". (Ahmad, Nasai).

A man came to the Prophet and said, ‘O Messenger of God! Who among the people is the most worthy of my good companionship? The Prophet said: Your mother. The man said, ‘Then who?’ The Prophet said: Then your mother. The man further asked, ‘Then who?‘ The Prophet said: Then your mother. The man asked again, ‘Then who?’ The Prophet said: Then your father. (Bukhari, Muslim).

You can find the above information anywhere, but the point I want to make is, that for a Muslim, the greatest desire they can have, is of paradise. we consider this life as a test and we go through hardships without losing our faith to get paradise. But, Prophet Muhammad rightly said “ Heaven is under the feet of your mother”, Allah valued the role of a mother so much.

In Islam, a woman is not entitled to do the domestic work. It might surprise you, but yes, forget about cooking for in-laws, a wife is not obliged to do any of the domestic work even for her husband’s supper. Away from general norms, a wife has full right to ask for her privacy whether you provide it in a joint family setting, or give her another home, that’s your concern. In Muslim homes, we don’t see these because the cultural norms have oversized the Islamic teachings.

Now the question is why the lopsided responsibilities are explicitly targeted to men, not women. In the above discussion, we find how women are favoured or honoured with some preferences.

it's lucid in the Quran that Allah has given some preferences over others. Allah kept this statement gender-neutral to show that women can also have preferences over men.

We can conclude that Islam values different roles of individuals differently. The value of a woman as a mother supersedes the value of her role as a wife .

There are several issues in which scholars of Islam have not reached a consensus. For a Muslim, Quran is infallible but interpretations are not. these discourses are not hidden from the world. There is a misconception that laws in Islam are not flexible and it's a rigid religion, but it's not true, there are enough debates and disagreements between scholars about ambiguous verses, sometimes they are affected by culture and perception. I conclude that I can't categorize Islam as patriarchy or matriarchy.

To some extent, it seems to be a macro-patriarchal micro-matriarchy, but it doesn't perfectly fulfil the criteria in totality.

Your thoughts:

III

Sexual division of labour

The question, why we have this sexual division of labour, and why only women are required to handle household chores, has become a hot topic in recent years. Some think that patriarchy has historically restricted women's movement indoors, while others argue that culture or traditions are to blame. So, let's analyze if this division is caused solely by the patriarchy or by something else.

According to anthropologist and archaeologist, Steven Kuhn of the University of Arizona, the sexual division of labour did not exist until the Upper Palaeolithic age and was only established recently in human history. It's possible that the sexual division of labour evolved to help humans acquire food and other resources more efficiently. We can see how vital division of labour is, for an industrial society in the work of French sociologist Emile Durkheim. However, there are various theories about the gendered division of labour. Some of them contradict one other, yet we can't deny that men and women have biological distinctions. The scientific name for physical differences between males and females of a species is "sexual dimorphism.". Many extreme examples exist: Peacocks far outclass peahens, for instance, while female anglerfish both outsize and outwit their tiny, rudimentary, parasitic male counterparts.

Men and women, unlike those animals, are more physiologically similar than we are different. However, there are a few fundamental differences in our anatomy. Some are suited to each sex's role in reproduction, while others are designed to help us identify each other distinct and aid in our mutual attraction. In general, men have higher muscle mass than women. Women's upper bodies are little over half as powerful as men's, and their lower bodies are around two-thirds as strong. Male and female bodies are well-designed for their respective roles. In ancient civilizations, sexual dimorphism played a role in affecting the division of labour. The traditional explanation of the sexual division of labour finds that males and females cooperate by targeting different foods. The emergence of cooking in early Homo may have created problems of food theft from women while the food was being cooked. As a result, females would recruit male partners to protect them and their resources from others. This concept, known as the theft hypothesis, accommodates an explanation as to why the labour of cooking is strongly associated with the status of women. Women are forced to gather and cook foods because they will not acquire food otherwise and access to resources critical for their reproductive success. On the contrary, men do not gather because their physical dominance allows them to scrounge cooked foods from women. Thus, women's foraging and food preparation efforts allow men to participate in the high-risk, high-reward activities of hunting.

It's obvious that men have an advantage in activities that entail physical exertion and risk. And it is for this reason that, even in the twenty-first century, men and women do not compete in the same sport. Men's and women's races exist, not men's versus women's races. No matter how much radical feminists try to endorse that men and women are identical, the fact is they are not. Here people misunderstand the word difference as "inferiority". In some characteristics, women are superior to men and vice versa. Psychologist Diane Halpern, PhD, a professor at Claremont College and past president (2005) of the American Psychological Association, points out that even where there are patterns of cognitive differences between males and females, "differences are not deficiencies." She continues, "Even when differences are discovered, we cannot conclude that they are irreversible," she says, "since the continual interplay of biological and environmental forces can change the amount and direction of the impacts at any time."

She is concerned about the evidence-based distinctions because she believes they are frequently exploited to justify prejudiced ideas and discriminatory behaviours towards girls and women. She advises anyone reading about gender disparities to assess if the differences are large enough to be important, as well as the interaction and influence of biological and environmental elements. There are also social, cultural, and patriarchal reasons for women being restricted to the home. They were treated as property and forced to restrictions.

I intentionally put these facto researched observations not to bore you up, but to make you aware of the differences and to understand that there is nothing wrong in the division of labour. But what about the sexual division of labour?

The reason we are discussing the sexual division of labour is that most of the opinion on this topic is based on the conception that, it's bad to have a sexual division of labour, which I would say is the consequence of a value-loaded analysis of outdoor and indoor work, and an implicit superiority of outdoor work over indoor work. There are many variables involved in deciding whether something is good or bad. In the discussion of the sexual division of labour, we will consider some variables as presumably good, like family, marriage, children, and finance. We must now strike a balance in our responsibilities in order to have a healthy marriage, a happy family, and healthy children. The link between mother and child is regarded as an atom or building block of society in numerous social studies. This isn't to say that men don't play a part in parenting. Men, too, have a significant influence on a child's behaviour. Single parenting is not a desirable family structure for both the parent and the children. These could be some of the most cliche justifications for women being increasingly active in domestic chores. But, even in today's environment, where there are a few options that can help women work outside, I will not deny that patriarchy has a role in confining women.

A 2019 report by the U.S. Bureau of Labour Statistics found that 49 per cent of women did housework daily, versus only 20 per cent of men, even if they were both employed. That indicates that there's still a lack of equality regarding domestic labour within the average American household, and it's a gap that might make marriage seem less advantageous for a career-oriented woman.

A working woman is a more subjugated version in females, in most cases, the woman has to complete the domestic work and then official work by herself. In the pursuit of women's empowerment, we have overburdened women with both fiscal and domestic responsibilities. (Again, there are exceptions where men completely take care of the household). So where is the problem? Most of the time we don't know the root cause of the issue. Do you think household works diminish someone as an individual? Indoor works are as important as outdoor works, but why do neither men nor women agree to associate themselves completely with it. Where does this difference come from?

If we psychologically believe, that household work is inferior or less valuable, neither of the sexes would agree to do it. For women empowerment, we only endorse women to outdoor work, do we think men would do the vice versa.

Why would men choose to do domestic work? There must be someone to take care of domestic work, whether it's male or female. Even if men are advantageous at outdoor work, but still, in contemporary society women are also perfectly capable of doing everything. It is now more important to have a strong brain than it is to have strong muscles. For both sexes, technology has produced a more fluid working environment. Some sociologists claim that patriarchy and fatherly love, which prioritises achievements, lead to inequality. But it is capitalism, not fatherly love, that is to blame. If we flip the order, placing more value on domestic work, the disproportionate privilege will automatically move from men to women. we can consider the tribes of Musou, Khasi, etc, these are the world's few matrilineal and matrilocal communities, where the value of domestic labour and reproductive roles is higher, and less influenced by capitalism. Although I do not believe in economic determinism, capitalism is responsible for the perception that outdoor or economic work is more desirable than unpaid domestic obligations. As a result, our society will be in conflict unless we address the value assigned to the division of labour. So before endorsing one gender to work in the prescribed or non-prescribed job, we must try to make efforts for a value-neutral division of profession.

Furthermore, the pay gap between men and women shows the average difference in aggregate incomes by gender; the lower average income of women might be due to a variety of factors. Even for the same job, women may face active discrimination in the workplace, as we observe in both the organised and unorganised sectors, there is a truth concerning wage discrimination. However, concluding that women get paid less primarily because of their gender is unreasonable, given males are more likely to travel, work longer hours, pursue high-risk positions, and retire late, resulting in their average income being higher.

Another factor in the income disparity could be the field and occupation chosen. You might say that the pattern in choice of occupation or sexual division of labour is a social construct. But the most developed countries which provide maximum social and economic equality, the number of men choosing STEM (Science Technology Engineering Mathematics) is far more than women. Since women in developing countries are socially and economically disadvantaged, they are more likely to gravitate toward STEM fields in order to climb up the career ladder and break the glass ceiling. However, as women's socioeconomic circumstances improve, they are more likely to gravitate toward non- STEM fields of study. This is called the gender-equality paradox. Recently, many social scientists have talked about the gender equality paradox in developed countries where women started choosing the field which is non-STEM(science technology engineering mathematics) where the pay is lesser as compared to the jobs in STEM.

The pink colourization of professions could be the next factor to consider. It refers to the high proportion of women in specific occupations. For example, doctors are paid more than nurses, while over 90% of nurses are female. Even though there are female doctors, they make less because of the pay system, which pays doctors based on the number of patients they see. Female doctors spend more time dealing with patients, which translates to less money. This act of prolonging interaction time has an underlying positive impact on doctor-patient engagement. I'm not denying that they can be discriminated against unfairly, but there are other reasons that have also been observed in studies.

In the case of the gender equality paradox, it's not the societal forces or patriarchy responsible for that, rather the amplified difference in the temperament of men and women when socioeconomic factors are suppressed by equality of opportunity.

Economic factor, American women's Football teams are paid very little as compared to the men, and the reason they gave is that the popularity and revenue generated is much lesser so they are paid less. Now, this is a valid reason from a capitalist perspective, but not a fair reason, as women work the same for a lesser reward. Now, we can compensate it from the aid by the government to increase the pay and spread awareness, and encourage the women's football game, so that it becomes equally popular.

Conclusion

A homemaker can be as empowered as the one doing a paid job or even more than her. In my opinion, if a woman is allowed and capable of making her own life decisions, she is empowered, despite the fact that this is a restrictive definition. A woman is empowered if she chooses to work for a living, and she is also empowered if she chooses to do domestic work. At its core, it is about the right to make choices. Now the question is why would anybody want to do household work, well many women and men love cooking and can do better in house management. The question itself is loaded with value judgment of work-type.

We must not presume in the first place, that a homemaker is oppressed and a paid working woman is liberated. It's probable that a woman who works in a company is more oppressed or objectified than a homemaker. There's is no doubt that financial stability can lead to women's empowerment. It is one of the important avenues but it's not the only avenue.

Endorsing women to hardship and making them use medication and surgery to alter and fit into the capitalist system is tyranny to their biology. One of the examples is the condition of female sugarcane workers in Maharashtra, who are suffering from barium exposure, which has resulted in a mass hysterectomy.

" If we want roles to have equal worth, we must show that they are equally significant."

As a society, we must first eliminate value prejudices against domestic work, and men doing cooking or dishes should be considered normal. This is the missing transitional phase in today's empowering process. We must strive towards value-neutral occupation before achieving gender-neutral economic division. Because domestic work is crucial and cannot be delegated to paid workers or helpers. Many people now argue that both husband and wife should work outside and the housework should be handled by a paid servant. This idea of both genders working in so-called professional jobs appears to be a good one. We can also speculate about its effect on the upbringing of children. However, this cannot apply to the lower classes, those who are less educated or who are destitute, this cannot be a universal solution.

So, if we want to create a grand theory, it should provide a solution to the majority of people, not just a few. So, what's the solution? Since value bias about work has been cultivated in people's minds for a long time, it will require some time to dispel. Value neutrality can first be instilled in the new generation's upbringing at home; this is the most critical step that will have a long-term impact. But for immediate results, few things can be done like free and compulsory education for girls, which can further push their age of marriage. At the very least, we can try to cook dinner together to limit the amount of time spent on domestic duties by one gender. A woman can share household chores with her husband and children, even if it's a small task. Men should aim to be more self-sufficient by performing their own chores. A good start could be taking the glass of water by yourself, don't tell her to do this stuff (it may sound insignificant, but believe me, these things are taboo in most Indian households), as a man wash your plates so that your children can observe and learn cooperation.

Recognize the worth of unpaid homework, which according to Oxfam research accounts for 40% of our GDP. Legislatively, domestic work can also be considered in GDP calculation, as domestic service is a major contribution to national development.

if we could define being a homemaker as an official occupation, women should be compensated for it by their husbands, just as their husbands are compensated by the firm. I understand that the husband would still retain financial authority, and in most situations, women would not be compensated. However, this step will have an impact on men's psychics, as they will realise that the service they had assumed was free is indeed not. The way few questions are asked in the census, how much a husband pays to his wife per month should also be asked.

These initiatives may appear light in comparison to the state's current attempts to generate a real result, but the psychology of men will undoubtedly be affected, forcing them to rethink their preconceived notions about domestic service. I believe that improving the value of a profession is preferable to encourage everyone to do the same in order to be considered valuable.

Islamic perspective

I am not an expert in Islam, but I have gathered some information from several sources. The division of labour is not explicitly mentioned in Islam. Marriage in Islam is an agreement between a man and a woman to spend the rest of their life together. Marriage, or nikah, is a literal handover of obligations from her father to her spouse. Her spouse would look after her in the same way as a girl's father does. A man is required to support his family by default. As a result, it's possible to call it a gendered division of labour. It's possible to argue that this is discrimination and a burden on men, but whether one likes it or not, this is the default system of financial responsibility. Now the question is, does that mean Islam prohibits women from pursuing a career? we have many examples in the history of Islam for example mother Khadija bint khuwaylid, the first wife of Prophet Mohammed(peace be upon him), was a rich businesswoman, who employed him. she was already a business tycoon. One more example is mother Aisha bint Abi Bakr (may Allah be pleased with her), when we think of top scholars of Islam after Prophet Mohammed (peace be upon him), the next name that comes to my mind is Aisha bint Abi Bakr (R.A.). She was the source of a quarter of rulings in Islamic laws. Here we are, struggling to give representation to women in legislation, but we forget how we got to know about a quarter of rulings from a woman. And it was not a forced representation without merit, she was a scholar of scholars (male) and was blessed with a sharp memory.

Women's bravery on the battlefield was demonstrated in the battle of Yarmouk against the Romans, One of the great woman generals was Khawla bint al-Azwar.

Even today, we rarely see a woman proposing to a man for marriage (directly or indirectly), but surprisingly, mother Khadija bint khuwaylid (R.A.) made the proposal to the prophet Mohammed (peace be upon him), and the only narration of marriage mentioned in the Quran is of Moses (peace be upon him), and it was the girl who directed her father for the marriage proposal. It's amazing to me that these two marriage stories have two things in common: first, both were initiated by empowered women, and second, both were hypergamous, since the prophet Mohammed (peace be upon him) was a shepherd and Moses was a refugee. In our society, generally, we consider men who work for their father-in-law or in-laws, to be unmasculine, but the story of Moses,(peace be upon him,) shows that there is no stigma associated with working for in-laws; rather, this incident of marriage defies the preconceived notion of masculine men. Marrying an older lady is likewise frowned upon in our community. In my life, I've rarely witnessed a young man marrying an older woman, let alone a divorcee. Prophet Mohammed's (peace be upon him) marriage, on the other hand, defies the stereotypes because he married a woman who was not only older than him but a widow. Imagine being a 25-year-old handsome man and marrying a much older widow.

And it all came about because they were both looking for honesty, modesty, and character. People criticise the prophet Muhammed for marrying several wives, but they never mention that he married widows and divorcees, which is still a taboo in modern culture, therefore historically there has been active participation of women in almost all the fields in Islam. so can a woman work and pursue her carrier?

Yes, a woman can work freely in Islam as long as she follows certain standards. She is permitted to work if the work ensures her chastity and honour. Does this imply that men are free to undertake any work they desire, without regard for chastity or honour? The answer is no. However, it is emphasised for women because women are the recipients or victims of the majority of workplace abuses and harassment. The Metoo movement is a great example. Does this imply that a woman can prioritise outdoor work over everything? In normal circumstances, I don't believe so, because, in Islam, a woman's motherly position is considerably greater and cherished more than any other employment role. If her job has a bearing on children's nurture and upbringing, she should prioritize her children first. It's conceivable if she can strike a balance between the two roles without compromising the motherly role. It's because a good upbringing determines the fates of many generations. A few decades ago, there was a trend in European countries where women were prioritizing their outdoor work over the motherly role by relying on alternatives, like opting for childcare centres and babysitters, breastfeeding was replaced by bottle feeding. Lactation in the United States had been declining in frequency but is apparently now undergoing a renaissance. Breastfed infants now appear to offer considerable advantages in terms of decreased rates of milk allergy, other allergies, and major infectious illnesses. Breastfeeding appears to facilitate mother-infant connection. The importance of the mother's involvement in the process of learning a first language. Loneliness, according to many sociologists, can be linked to the early mother-child interaction, despite the fact that few studies have been conducted in this area. So there's no denying how important a mother's early involvement is for a child.

We generally see in our society how women are confined to household work. Not only that, this could have been justified as a division of labour, but some men generally marry with the expectation that his wife will cook, do laundry, and clean for them and their entire family. But, contrary to popular belief, a woman is not entitled to perform any of it under Islam. Forget about cooking for in-laws; a wife is not obligated to do any domestic work, even preparing her husband's supper. It may be upsetting to some men, but it is the truth. The care of your parents is solely on your shoulder. Don't expect it from any other person, even if it's your wife. If your mom is facing difficulty in work, then you should assist her, if you are unable to, you should hire a maid or assistant. If your wife is assisting and taking care of your mother, she is doing you and your family a favour and charity.

So, Islamically if she does justice to her obligations(which primarily include the care of children) then she can definitely work, and she can also work in odd circumstances. And what's more remarkable is that whatever she earns will be hers to keep. Nobody, including her spouse, can take from that. But it's a favour if she wants to spend money on her spouse or family (or if she wishes to buy you dessert). The burden of maintenance falls on the husband, regardless of how wealthy a woman is. That's something he can't complain about. It's OK if the woman chooses to share the financial burden, but it'll be her decision, not anyone else's. On the other hand, a woman owes certain responsibilities to her husband, such as caring for her children (this does not mean that men are exempted from this responsibility), guarding her modesty when her husband isn't home, etc. There is a disagreement between scholars that whether she should take her husband's consent to do a job or not. According to some experts, because it will affect the dynamics of their relationship, hence consent is required, another group of scholars say, if she's fulfiling her obligations, she shouldn't take permission or consent. In Islam marriage is a contract and in that contract, a woman can insert any clause or condition, she can write it on the contract whether she wishes to work or study after she gets married. If the guy agrees, great; if not, the marriage will be called off.

We can deduce from the preceding talks that there is no rigid structure for any division of labour in Islam. However, there are recommended roles and obligations towards relationships, for both genders which is inclined towards the conventional sexual division of labour. You might be wondering if all of these things are covered by Islamic law, why Saudi Arabia places so many limitations on women. Many elements influence a country's legislation, such as the economy, patriarchy, culture, history, colonialism, and so on, because no country follows Sharia or Islamic rules in its entirety. Saudi Arabia recently granted women driving rights, which is odd, given the fact that women used to ride horses throughout Islamic history. As men dominate most of the contemporary pivotal positions in the religious arena, thus no matter how objective the teachings of the Quran and Prophet Mohammed (peace be upon him) are, there is always a fear of patriarchy sneaking into interpretations. The good news is that any scholarly ruling may be reviewed to see if it is consistent with the Quran and Sunnah. The matter with ambiguity has been progressively debated and discussed among scholars, but those discussions are failed to be cultivated in Muslim society. Religious education is critical, not only for Muslims but for people of all faiths, so that all segments of society can internalise the soul message and avoid becoming tangled in ignorance.

Your thoughts:

IV
Attraction

Pre-requisite

I've centred my analysis in this chapter on "social interaction and orientation," which is distinct from mere "action". Social interactions are the acts, behaviours, or practises of two or more individuals who are mutually oriented towards each other's selves, i.e., any activity that strives to influence or take into consideration each other's subjective experiences or goals. The behaviour of the rapist and the victim does not constitute social interaction if the victim is considered as a physical object, nor does the behaviour of the guard and the prisoner, the torturer and the tormented. [Reference: Understanding Conflict And War: Vol. 2:The Conflict Helix Chapter 9 Social Behavior And Interaction By R.J. Rummel].*

We currently live in a society where "attention" is a major source of concern for everyone. As a result, looking "attractive" has turned into a requirement. I used the word "attractive" in the sense of "being easily noticeable." It's not just for sexual attraction. Attractiveness refers to everything that makes a person more desirable for a career, relationship, or other endeavours. We shouldn't presume that just because someone wants to look attractive, they're a playboy or a playgirl.

We've seen people rationalizing crimes against women by blaming their dress or independence. Others, on the other hand, rejected their argument entirely, stating that men are solely to blame for their repulsive mindset. So, rather than being influenced by emotion, political correctness, or liberal pressure, I opted to research this matter academically. I'm not referring to rape or other forms of violence against women. I'd choose to talk about one of the most basic aspects of human behaviour, which is "attraction." According to multiple studies, facial symmetry and the contrast between various parts of the face, such as lips and eyelashes, and the skin, determine the beauty of a woman's face. This is why we have cosmetics to help us perform these tasks. As a result, I began interviewing men and women on a number of themes linked to attraction in order to better understand the effects of attraction on both genders. When I questioned guys why they go to the gym, they said they go to relieve stress, strengthen themselves, and many said, to look attractive with a good physique. The majority of the time, you'll get straightforward replies. Similarly, if you ask a man about his appearance, I have never seen a man who is reluctant to admit that they dress to be more attractive.

Once, I asked a female friend that why she wears makeup.

(Sometimes, my curious mind has cost me friendships, don't try this if you are deeply single)

She replied that " it makes her feel confident and she likes it ". It wasn't a satisfactory explanation for a logical person like me, so I dared to dig a little deeper, but she got irritated, and our conversation ended up with heated arguments. Some things are difficult to explain. But, if love, the most complicated emotion, can be explained partially with logic, why not this? When I asked the same questions to the girls, I received mixed responses; many stated it was because they loved it or felt confident in it, while a few hinted it was to make them look attractive. But mostly they used terms like confidence, liking, etc.

As I know, Confidence does not appear on its own; it requires a solid foundation. You can't feel confident merely because you exist, confidence is there in terms of intelligence, attractiveness, competence, and so on. According to sociologists and psychologists, there are two main reasons why women apply makeup and dress in particular ways.

In terms of camouflage, Women who are worried or insecure may use makeup to camouflage themselves and appear less noticeable. In addition, women are more likely than men to engage in "Same-Sex Aggression".

For Seduction, women who want to appear more confident, gregarious, and assertive use makeup to make themselves appear more attractive.

According to the Association for Psychological Science, attractive people are treated better in many aspects of life, including dating, employment, and criminal trials (source scienceofpeople.com). "I feel this topic has a sociological, historical, biological, and psychological answer—an answer in numerous elements of gender studies and fashion trends," says Reshma Khan, a sociologist. People are drawn toward increasingly provocative and revealing attire, which is a significant motif in today's women's fashion. The proportion of fabric to the skin has dropped considerably as more women wear revealing clothing that exposes their bodies to the point of near-nakedness".

You might be thinking, 'You already know all of this, so why am I making a big deal about it?' It's because the majority of women are either oblivious or deny it by rephrasing with terms like "liking" or "confidence". This defensive stance of women is justified because, if a woman explicitly affirms these reasons, we as a society judge their character. In many cases, a person unknowingly follows a model or actor and attempt to imitate them, and this is sometimes done to avoid same-sex hostility. This is also true when it comes to dressing. The reason I created this background is to emphasise, that sometimes, a woman or a man may intentionally or unconsciously desire to be judged by their appearance.

Is it women to blame for provoking men?

When we argue that molesting a woman is justified because she is sexually attractive, it's like blaming a rich person for being robbed; thus, this argument is already flushed and can be deemed disgusting.

(I request you to have this in your mind while going through the below discourse. I'll try to keep reminding you that if someone is attractive, regardless of gender, he or she is not asking to be molested.)

But, while some may argue that it is men's ill mentality, and women should be free to wear anything they want. This basically translates as, even if a man encounters a naked lady, he must not stare at her, because if he does he has an ill mentality.

We've seen these arguments before in this debate, yet they're undiagnosed. Because we debate on opposite extremes without taking into account the fact, that sexual interaction cannot be observed in isolation.

"Why is it bad if a man stares at you?" I asked one of my friends. A man does not have a laser weapon in his eyes, thus he is not physically harming you, and you would be unaware if you didn't spot him gazing. What makes it a crime, then? (It can land you in jail in our country if you don't know.)

"Because that would make her feel uncomfortable," she replied. I then asked her to elaborate, to which she said that it's tough to do so, but it's uncomfortable when someone looks at you in a sexualizing manner.

I agreed with her and then asked, how would you know if he is staring at you "in a sexualizing way"?

"I can sense it " she replied.

This raised some of the questions in my mind.

What if a man feels uncomfortable because a half-naked girl is seated next to him? When a girl in revealing clothes come closer or approaches, many men become highly uncomfortable. Is it OK for men to be uncomfortable in that situation? Ask yourself, Are men allowed to feel uncomfortable in that situation?

One counter-argument could be, in the first case, a man is objectifying a woman by his eyes that might have a psychological impact on a woman, which makes her uncomfortable, so the cause is man's action and the effect is discomfort in the woman.

So, according to that logic, one can argue that, when a woman sexualizes herself, certain body parts of women trigger the biological instinct of men to reproduce, which manifests as the action of "staring." In this case, the woman affected the man's behaviour and state of mind through the same channel of sexual interaction. (when I say it affects men, it does not mean it gives license to molest. That's why at the beginning of this chapter I clarified that, this dialect would be about interaction and orientation, not mere actions.)

Some questions for you to think about: Will a half-naked man approaching a woman make her feel uncomfortable? If that's the case, why can't a man feel uncomfortable when interacting with a half-naked woman? Why is the clause about outraging one's modesty only applied to women and not to men? Should a woman who stares at a man with six-pack abs and a seductive physique be labelled as ill-minded or characterless? Can a shirtless man on the street complain to an officer about an infringement on his modesty, if he is stared at by women on the street?

This is because of the faulty conception of attraction, in which modesty and virginity are associated with women, not men. So either they believe that men are invincibly modest or they don't have it at all.

One could argue that the type of "discomfort" experienced by women differs. I agree with you, but how can we judge one gender's discomfort as outrageous while not the other?

Is there a difference in the intensity of discomfort felt by a man surrounded by half-naked women and a woman surrounded by half-naked men? The only difference one can point out is the element of threat that can affect women more than men. If we eliminate the factor of fear from her discomfort, will a woman accept this behaviour as not offensive?

Because the word uncomfortable or discomfort is so abstract, we can't judge and scale who to hold accountable. if someone wants to argue that a woman is not intentionally sexualizing rather it is men's ill nature, then I would ask " Are you not aware of this biological phenomenon of attraction?

Although a woman or a man may not wish to exhibit those consequences, the latent impacts cannot be ignored intellectually or scientifically ". Another phrase that you may have heard in Hindi is "tumahri Nazar kharab hai." This argument assumes that only men objectify women, however, this is not the case. Take a look at any supermarket magazine rack, and you'll notice that women are commonly the subject of sexual objectification. New research suggests that the brain processes female images differently than male images, adding to this trend. Women are more likely to be picked apart by the brain and perceived as parts rather than wholes, according to research published online on June 29 in the European Journal of Social Psychology. Men, on the other hand, are considered as a whole, not as a collection of parts. "Every day, ordinary women are reduced to their sexual body parts," said Sarah Gervais, co-author of the study and a psychologist at the University of Nebraska, Lincoln. "It's not just supermodels who have to deal with this." The results revealed a significant disparity in men's and women's pictures. When viewing female images, participants were better at recognising specific parts of female photos than they were at matching whole-body photographs to the originals. When it came to male images, the opposite was true: people could recognise a man as a whole more easily than his individual pieces. Individual female body parts were also better distinguished than individual male body parts, supporting the local processing or objectification that was taking place.

"Both men and women do this to women, "So don't hold it against the men here " Gervais stated.

(July 24, 2012) (By Stephanie Pappas)

To tackle this issue, the idea that males have a bad mentality (tumhari Nazar khrab hai) is not very appropriate.

According to the findings of the preceding studies, "attraction" is an intriguing phenomenon that affects both genders and is widely employed by capitalists and corporations for marketing and sales.

Is this to say that staring isn't a bad thing?

It may appear like the preceding discussion is attempting to demonstrate this, but it is not. Although it is possible that staring at someone in a disturbing manner is immoral and not acceptable as social etiquette. Criminalising this behaviour is a point of contention among people, researchers, and governments. In terms of what constitutes sexual harassment, different countries have differing views. In some countries, staring at certain body parts of women is considered sexual harassment and in some, it is not. It is interesting that in Britain, telling a woman a sex joke is more offensive than putting arms around the waist. In Norway, Sweden and Denmark, starring at certain body parts of women is considered harassment by nearly 25-30 per cent of people. But it is considered harassment in France and Britain. (source DW.com on sexual harassment in Europe).

So, when there is a plurality of opinion and lack of consensus on what should be labelled sexual harassment, sentencing people to prison for gazing could be problematic. Even if we want to punish persons who stare abruptly, we must ensure that justice is served equally to both men and women. I am not sure about the criminalisation of staring, but at least there should be a social toll on those who commit this action.

Now, I would introduce you to a concept what I call "responsibility of sexual interaction". I believe that the "responsibility of sexual interaction is on the shoulders of both men and women". It means one sex can't completely blame the other sex for any kind of sexual interaction. (Interaction vs action, I hope you must have read the prerequisite for this chapter)

My whole deduction will be on justifying the theory "responsibility of sexual interaction". If you agree with this conception then you can skip the below discussion and continue reading from the double-asterisk **

Insidiously, It has become a fashion, the more revealing cloth one wears, the more we consider the person empowered. This conception can be majorly seen with respect to women. When we are told to imagine a successful or empowered man, it might appear in a tuxedo, but let's imagine a successful woman, in our mind it comes a woman in a skirt or in a dress which is similar to that of a man, like pants shirts. It might be because of Western influences, but we can't ignore the sexualization of dress in women. In men, we have a limited scope of sexualization in dressing. This makes me think of one more question, should the use of attraction be allowed to influence the consequences?

Hypothetically, Won't it be discriminatory to allow women to dress seductively, but males to be totally covered in an interview dominated by male interviewers? We may also conceive a scenario in which a shirtless male with a nice enticing physique influences a women-dominated interview panel. As a result, there's a good chance that the interviewee's attire can influence the outcomes. However, there is a counter-argument that it is easier for a man to get employed in a core capitalist system than it is for a woman. It could be due to the maternity and ethical costs of hiring a woman over a man; in other words, a business owner would never want to pay for maternity benefits and leave for a non-working employee, in this case, a woman.

The presence of women creates a covert burden for their security, especially in a society where every hour a woman is molested or abused. So their attractiveness should be allowed to influence a job interview to compensate for the disadvantaged position of a woman in a capitalist system. Today's patriarchy as objectification of women is assisted by capitalism. There is no quantifiable data to do the comparative analysis, so I'll leave it up to you to contemplate.

**continue

Don't worry if you're having trouble understanding. The purpose of the foregoing study is to demonstrate to all of us that both sexes are responsible for sexual attraction. It's what I refer to as "the theory of sexual interaction."

One cannot entirely absolve themself of sexual responsibility and place the blame for any interaction between them, on others. You might argue that by adopting this theory, I am condoning rape as the victim's fault. the answer is NO. There have been several studies on rape and its causes, and researchers agree that rape is more than just a sexual act; it is profoundly linked to many variables such as rage, dominance, sadism, including sexual gratification and so on. Sexual violence is one of the outcomes of dominance that can draw its origin from patriarchy and matriarchy. There are different kinds of rapes and perpetrators. When it happens to a young woman and young man, we can speculate about sexual attraction, but we can't explain why it happened to a child or an elderly woman. Similarly, according to statistics, the perpetrator in the majority of rape cases is a close one of the victim, such as her boyfriend, husband, best friend, or other close relatives. As a result, a woman is more vulnerable within her home than she is outside. It's also true that hostility is lower in these situations than when done by a stranger. However, it is a psychological manifestation of dominance that may be seen in many animals. Rapes driven by rage, domination, sadism, and toxic masculinity have nothing to do with clothing, one who is fully covered can also be raped just like those who are half-naked.

So this theory of sexual interaction deals with the "orientation" of males and females, not the "action". As rape comprises of coercive sexual "action", Sexual interaction could be the first step to further coercion but only when it's motivated by sexual gratification not by anger, dominance, sadism, etc. Sexual orientation towards the opposite gender is present in all straight sexes, but it doesn't mean one should be allowed to act on it. It's normal to feel attracted just like we feel anger, hunger, sleep, etc but we are not allowed to act on it every time. That's why we don't accept incest and not normal sexual behaviour to manifest in our society even if the orientation is associated with it. So before making any extreme statement like " She was raped because she was provoking " Or " It's all men's ill mentality ", we should not forget our sexual responsibility of attraction. And this is the only way out, or else this debate will never end, if we ride on extremes the end result would be the same, so it's better to take a middle way to acknowledge the strength and weaknesses of different genders and take our responsibility of interaction.

Islamic perspectives

In Islam, modesty is compulsory for both men and women. It is one of our core essentials in our beliefs. There is no discrimination or unequal judgement on modesty.

It starts from covering our body parts, but it has more deep and more layered understanding. Modesty is not limited to being and looking modest to others. It has an underlying connotation of being modest to ourselves. There are horizontal strata of modesty which starts with

- Dressing,
- Nonverbal: it refers to how you carry yourself in front of others, which includes posture, body language, walking manner, and so on.
- verbal: it refers to how we communicate with each other, particularly with those of the opposite gender. Let's start with a definition of the term "mahram," which refers to those you can't marry, such as your mother, father, siblings, etc. In Islam, incest is forbidden, although cousin marriages are permitted. It means we can't hang around with our cousins (of the opposite gender, of course), as we can with our consanguineal siblings.

When it comes to mahram and non-mahram, our interactions are very different. We as Muslims are judged on a stricter scale. Is our conversation with non-mahram formal or informal? and if it is informal, to what extent is it informal? If we flirt and try to seduce the opposing gender, we are engaging in immodesty. You're probably wondering how we'd choose our life partners if we couldn't even date or hang out together. (Marriage will be explored in the upcoming subtopic).

Due to physiological differences, the extent of clothing may differ between men and women. For men and women, the aura of attraction is distinct. The Quran and Prophet

Muhammed's (PBUH) teachings encourage men and women to be modest. As we all know, the crime of adultery has a severe punishment in Islam, yet it is equally inflicted on both men and women. In this way, Islam imposes a responsibility on both men and women to maintain modesty and mutual respect. By placing god, or Allah, at the centre of the world and human action, the right to command has been transferred from society and men, to the divine being, Allah. This means that men are not responsible for correcting the dressing of any women; rather, Allah has commanded that we dress or act in a certain way so that we do not wrong ourselves.

It's worrisome that another person can violate our modesty, but the greater danger is eroding our own modesty. There are a variety of ways to go about doing this. We outrage our modesty with our eyes if we watch something that is forbidden, such as a movie that is vulgar, starring a girl or watching pornographic content. Listening to any vulgar content or defamation about others would be a violation of our ear's modesty. Similarly, abusing or slandering someone violates the modesty of our tongue. Talking about Our prophet Muhammad (peace be upon him),

One of the narration goes like this." "He was shier than a virgin in her boudoir. When he hates a thing we read it on his face. He does not stare at anybody's face. He always casts his eyes down. He looks at the ground more than he looks sky-wards. His utmost looks at people are glances." (Bukhari 1/504)

Modesty is a simplified translation of the word "haya".

Prophet indicated: "Every way of life has an innate character. The character of Islam is haya. Modesty is an integral part of faith, modesty in behaviour, interaction with people, actions.

The importance of modesty doesn't end here. Our prophet Muhammad (peace be upon him) was modest, even with the other men around him, modesty is also a sign of respect to others and ourselves.

Your thoughts:

V

Marriage

In contemporary society, there is a discussion over arranged and love marriages. I'm not going to debate over which method is the best. I'll attempt to give you an ideal type of both types of marriages.

There are some pros and cons of both systems. In an arranged marriage, you are more judged by your face value than your intrinsic value. Both the parties would trust their parents and relatives for the right choice in the beginning. They first look at the manifested conduct and character of the individual. They make sure about the background, lineage, status and wealth of the family. These are very crucial sources, if you want to see the real conduct of a person, observe the way he or she treats the people in blood relations like mother and father.

The individuals value the perspectives of family members and others in the immediate vicinity in order to gain a better understanding of the individual. The flow of decisions is inverted pyramidical. Individuals are given the opportunity to have the final say after the approval of the family members. Two families are actively involved in all stages of marriage, resulting in strong social cohesion. In an arranged marriage, there are two extremes of pros. In this, even a person with no sense of humour, less charisma, and less confidence can get a woman he couldn't have wooed easily. And a woman who is attractive enough and possesses feminine characteristics but lacks accomplishments or ambition can easily attract a well-off, financially successful man. Arranged marriage ensures a favourable macro environment for a girl, but can't guarantee the micro relation with the husband.

The cons can be lack of individuals saying and authority in marriage, sometimes individual agrees for the sake of his or her parent's happiness.

This frequently results in forced marriages. This type of marriage is ideal for those who don't have specific expectations or who have set such a high bar that no one can meet, and who haven't met someone with whom they can envision themselves in a long-term relationship such as marriage, i.e. sexually introverted people. And this is a very natural and normal choice that many people make later in life.

Now, when it comes to love marriage, Before we define love marriage, we must first define love. To put it simply, love is the extreme form of liking. We sometimes discover it after spending a lot of time with someone, and sometimes we can tell right away whether or not we can live with the person. This can be affected by certain qualities and traits of the person, that we are attracted to. Love marriage is a decisive derivative of compatibility based on liking. It has a pyramidal flow of decision-making authority that flows from the individual to the parents at last. Individuals have complete decision-making authority, but this is also one of the disadvantages because sometimes adolescents, in their infatuation, take actions that are harmful to them and their families. However, I would not engage in a discussion about the ideal age for marriage because neither science nor Islam provides us with this information. The only thing I can say in favour of love marriage is that regretting our decisions is preferable over blaming our parents for poor selection.

Following that, love marriages dismantle the Endogamy barrier and encourage tolerance and acceptance in society.

As there are numerous advantages to love marriage, there is a group of people who believe that arranged marriage is a horrible idea and that love marriage is the only way to go. So, I began to study the data. For convenience, I went to the "Compare camp" an online site, where you can see their data, They have analysed more than 25 research papers on marriage and stated the below statistics.

In Europe, there were an estimated 2.2 million marriages and nearly 1 million divorces in 2016. Infidelity is one of the major causes of divorces. Around 45% in the US(2018) and 54.9% in Sweden(2002), of first marriages, ended up in divorce. The divorce rate has been increasing in Europe.

Firstly, divorce is not evil but not a virtue as well, as it destroys many lives and especially affects children. But sometimes marriage itself becomes death to individuals, it's a way out of any toxic relationship. But the reason I am presenting the above statistics to highlight that, in European countries, there is no concept of arranged marriage. They know only one process of marriage that is love, their definition of love is very different from what we consider love in Indian culture. Premarital and extra-marital intimacy is not taboo in those countries. But still, we can see the humongous numbers of divorces in those nations. When we see the top five countries, we have the Maldives is the country with the highest divorce rate followed by Belarus and the US.

We can observe that divorce rates are high in both types of countries where love marriage is common and where it is frowned upon. When we talk about countries where arranged marriage is common, we may deduce from the system that there is a reasonable chance of divorce. However, why is the divorce rate so high in places where arranged marriages are not common? There could be a number of reasons for this, including a lessening in the stigma associated with divorce and women feeling more empowered to make decisions. But we'll never be able to explain why two people who were together for years before marriage and know almost everything about each other got divorced. When I was researching this issue, one example that sprang to mind was a beautiful relationship between two South Indian artists, Naga Chaitanya and Samantha Akkineni. You may have heard of them, but if you haven't, let me tell you that they had a beautiful love story. However, the pair recently acknowledged that their four-year relationship is over. The soon-to-be-divorced couple has decided to stay friends but pursues their own paths. I'm not sure about the reasons, but they were well acquainted. I'm not using this example as an ideal type because I don't want to fall prey to any authoritative or straw man fallacies. But the above data of separation implies that there is something else that is equally vital in a marriage partnership. In order to marry, individuals sometimes defy their parents. However, this undermines the couple's support from the family institution during fallback and attrition in marriage.

The point I'm trying to convey is that we shouldn't be disgusted by arranged marriages, as love marriages are also not the guaranteed path to salvation.

Both marriage systems play an important role, depending on the individual's preference. As a result, we can conclude that it is not only significant how much you know about someone, but also how much we don't know about one other. Knowing everything about someone isn't always a good idea; we're wired to be bored. Consider anything in the world; if you do it every day, monotonously, you will eventually become bored. According to psychology, a little mystery is an aphrodisiac. Because the majority of the time in an arranged marriage, the entire person is a mystery, it fosters a desire to learn more about each other. And by the time they've learned the majority of the things, they've already established a family and a long history, which reinforces the bond. The main risk with arranged weddings is that it is sometimes too late to realise that staying with this person is impossible, which can lead to divorce. However, in love marriages, the element of mystery is typically absent, and the excitement fades with time. this absence of mystery can lead to a stable relationship, but people can get bored with one other, especially if their partners don't keep things interesting. So, in both cases, it is entirely dependent on each individual's effort and commitment to each other.

Meanwhile, online dating sites and mobile apps such as Tinder and alternatives of marriage such as live-in relationships have made marriage seems to be an option,

(A live-in relationship is different from marriage in many ways but in a foundational definition, Generally, psychologists have a consensus that live-in relationships are associated with freedom, both tend to have their own space as no obligations or responsibilities and less commitment are involved. Both individuals can keep the status as single.)

But no matter how much one argues against marriage, it can't be denied that it's an integral part of forming a family and women's reproductive security, which are essential for the survival of the human race.

Islamic perspective

You can only know so much about a person; the human brain and behaviour is the most intricate subject matter; we don't even know who we are. According to the "looking glass self" theory, "you perceive yourself as the rest of the world sees you." Many psychologists believe that we will never be able to fully comprehend or define how an individual thinks, or what memories that individual may have, or how those memories contribute to who they are. The point I'm trying to make is that we, as "others," will never fully comprehend a human being, just as we haven't really comprehended ourselves.

Does this imply that a boy should choose anyone who appears to be a girl as a partner? Ehmm, No, we are not mechanical engineers. Islam is a natural progression that focuses on the concept of the middle path. It is acknowledged that no one can find a perfect in this life; we all have flaws and bad habits, and there is no such thing as a perfect soul or partner. it means that no matter how hard you look, you will never discover someone who is perfect. It is our obligation to make the relationship perfect, which implies that every marriage can be perfect.

Is Islam against Love marriages? No, rather the first marriage of prophet Muhammed (PBUH) with mother

Khadija bint khuwaylid (R.A.) can be said a love marriage. Many similarities exist between Prophet Muhammed's (PBUH) marriage and love marriage. Khadija bint khuwaylid (R.A) was a businesswoman who hired prophet Muhammed (PBUH) for work. She had previously turned down many marriage proposals from high-status men of that time. She didn't require a husband to look after her financial needs. And Muhammad did not have the means to seek a wife and was not declared a prophet yet. But she liked the honesty, modesty, charisma, truthfulness and dedication of this man, Muhammed.

So She sends him the proposal for the marriage. The rest of the story you can read anywhere. So, if this isn't a love marriage, what is it? For the sake of argument, if I agree that it's not the kind of love marriage that we understand today, even then I can surely say, this marriage was not an arranged one. So it's obvious that marriage of your choice is allowed in Islam, even if you don't call it a love marriage.

According to Islamic tradition, you should try your best to get to know someone. Love marriage is all about compatibility. When you first realize that you like someone and that you have a strong sense of compatibility with him or her, inform a friend or family member to learn more about them. Pay attention to how he or she treats his or her family members; if you witness a person degrading or humiliating his or her family members, it's a red flag because there's a good possibility he or she will treat you the same way in the future.

We are allowed to meet the person a number of times, but only with parental permission and supervision. We can meet the individual as many times as we need to understand compatibility, but not in the corner of a room with no one else around, and obviously, not in an OYO room, the meeting should be in a public place.

You could think that these approaches are idealistic and that they are impossible to accomplish with Asian parents. However, the difficulty with Muslim households is that we tend to go to extremes. On the one hand, there are those, who are so rigid that they won't even allow their son to see the girl's face before marriage, while on the other hand, other parents don't mind their children doing anything, including premarital intimacy. There are several factors making marriage difficult such as financial constraints, a man without a career, unreasonable material and qualitative expectations, and others. That is why Islam makes marriage easy. Those who are afraid of marriage because of their financial conditions.

Allah says in the Quran "*And marry the unmarried among you and the righteous among your male slaves and female slaves. If they should be poor, Allah will enrich them from His bounty, and Allah is all-Encompassing and Knowing.*" [24:32]

You may think, that early marriage would stop people from being career-oriented and divert them to focus on the relationship. To some extent, it can be true but the end results can be debated, whether a marriage would eliminate the irrelevant sexual distraction from a person or it will burden him or her with responsibility. But from an Islamic perspective, huge wealth is not a success. Rather this life is a test and those who strive to be best in whatever the qualities they are endowed with by Allah and hold his or her belief, are successful. The spirit of capitalism is absent in Islam, but the spirit of meritocracy and philanthropy is there in one form or another.

Those who are capable enough should not delay marriage.

"The Messenger of Allah said: 'O young men, whoever among you can afford it, let him get married, for it is more effective in lowering the gaze and guarding chastity, and whoever cannot then he should fast, for it will be a restraint (wija') for him.'" [Sunan an-Nasa'I, 3209]

In this context, the Prophet (peace and blessings be upon him) said, *"If someone with whose piety and character you are satisfied comes to you, then marry him. If you do not do so, there will be disorder in the earth and a great deal of evil."*

The most important thing is, the criteria of selecting a life partner was made clear by mentioning the primary intrinsic qualities to look in a person, and then to look to secondary qualities that are wealth, lineage, beauty etc. Soboth the qualities are recommended with the hierarchy of priority. And these primary questions can be tested to some extent by looking at the person, how he or she treats the family members and those who are less in order of power. This way we can at least get an idea of compatibility and whether it's conceivable to spend life with that person or not.

Supplementary discussion

Most of the time we expect an improved version of our partner and we try to change them. But, it's recommended to consider that the person you are going to marry will be the same for your entire life. And it solves many problems, example if a man is addicted to cigarettes and if a woman marries him expecting him to change, let's say a girl who wears jeans and a t-shirt but after marriage, she is forced to or expected to wear a saree or something more acceptable in our society, a working woman is expected to leave her work after marriage, etc. these expectations to alters someone's behaviour after marriage is not Islamic. Yes, if one changes for good by one's wish, it is good. But we can't force someone to get moulded the way we want. we must marry a person, expecting him or her to not to change, this will lighten the mutual expectations. If you hate Cigarettes don't marry a smoker hoping your love would change him or her, you may succeed, but the odds are stacking against you. If you marry a working woman, you have no right to forbid her from working; if you don't want her to work, tell her before marriage, or accept her as she is. If a girl marries a low-income man with the hope that he will become wealthy in the future, she should not place her hopes and aspirations in him; perhaps he will earn more, or both of you can share the expenses, but if not, the relationship will suffer.

Your thoughts:

VI

Why women the honour?

Every year, hundreds of women are murdered by their families in the name of "honour." Honour killings are difficult to quantify since they often go undetected, the perpetrators go unpunished, and the concept of family honour justifies the conduct in some cultures.

Honour killings have been reported in Bangladesh, the United Kingdom, Brazil, Ecuador, Egypt, India, Israel, Italy, Jordan, Pakistan, Morocco, Sweden, Turkey, and Uganda, according to reports submitted to the United Nations Commission on Human Rights. Some countries refuse to submit the report at all. I've always wondered why it's so common all around the world. The same question arises as to why honour is only associated with women, not men. Why is it that we penalise a woman for Exogamy but rarely a man? Honour can be the source of many evils that still exist in our culture, including honour killing. There are various ills associated with the concept of honour, such as forced marriage and unwanted restrictions, but the most extreme form is honour killing. By looking up at these reports many questions arise, that if we look from a Conservative perspective as well, why only women are the honour. Families should be equally offended by a man's conduct if we truly cherish chastity.

Female morality and virginity, which are established in social customs, are closely related to a family's honour. Honour violence is a form of patrilineal gender roles manifestation. There's a way in which a woman's worth is exclusively determined by her physical appearance, sexuality, and ability to reproduce Honour. Honour culture has traditional traits, and according to certain studies, it is more prevalent in less developed countries with poorer human capital. (Critelli & Willett, 2012; Kulwicki, 2002).

Honour serves as social capital and insurance in the absence of economic wealth or a powerful welfare state. In a poor welfare state, the family's network has no choice but to rely on reputation and honour to survive. You'll need the correct connections to assist you with day-to-day tasks. As a result, a loss of honour makes life more difficult. The findings reveal that in tribal collective communities, honour serves as a substitute for the welfare system, leading to the conclusion that "so-called" honour violence and honour culture are linked to poverty and socioeconomic concerns. In order to retain a good reputation and family honour, people are under a lot of pressure to obey social and cultural standards, which also legitimise violence as a form of discipline. (Badayneh, 2012; Erez & Berko, 2010).

When there is a strong economic foundation, honour values become less significant, but they will continue to have an impact on family lives until the entire population reaches the same socioeconomic level. The presence of honour killings in rich countries is apparent that there are other factors responsible. The other factors could be deduced from the patrilineal system of heritage. Religion could also be used to justify honour killings. Her purity is almost inextricably linked to her chastity. She had to be pristine and abecedarian till the day she married. (Ouis, 2009). Honour violence can also be considered as a product of patriarchy and propertization of women.

Virginity

Honour also manifests as purity, as in our culture being a virgin is considered a virtue and thing of pride. This false sense of pride and honour is hypocritically confined to the purity of women, not men. This also points towards an idea of patriarchal control and regulation over women. This can be a major reason for honour and gender-grounded violence.

In our country, as in western society, there is a growing trend that says if you're a virgin, you're a loser. This has surfaced substantially because of the hypocrisy in our culture that virginity is only associated with women, not men. Some issues raised by feminists are not for the purpose of empowerment, but to chase men in all the spheres, irrespective of good or bad, to ensure equality. It's like, why should men have all the fun. For instance, smoking, drinking, alcohol, abusive language and so on. These are certainly not good for anyone, but some women see them as empowerment since, historically men have been free to do whatever they want, while women have been restricted simply because they aren't "The Men." This is also true when it comes to virginity. Men are not regarded immoral in any manner for having multiple partners, but women are harshly judged. This association of virginity to women is grounded on a defective conception of intimacy or intercourse. This defective conception is still used in the ultramodern world and leads to the legislation of discriminative laws against men and women.

In this conception, during the process of intercourse, it's abstractly presumed, that men are on the receiving and women are on the losing end.

This defective generality of intimacy where we feel that only men are in the receiving end, not the women, was extensively misused in and around the globe. When two consenting adolescents involve in intimacy, all the time it's the boy, who used to get penalized for sexual offences.

One example is a landmark decision by Justice N Anand Venkatesh of the Madras High Court, who stated that "penalising a teenage boy who enters into a relationship with a young girl by treating him as a lawbreaker was noway the objective of the POCSO Act." It cannot be denied that the Madras High Court, in this landmark decision, has accurately acknowledged that the POCSO Act is often abused by families to execute their teenage daughters' boyfriends. That is why I stated that this faulty generality is harmful to both men and women. Although the illustration below isn't a perfect one, it surely finds its root in that. This is the biggest reason why we can not conceive of men being raped by a woman, we never conceive its possibility because purity is always associated with women and only she can lose it!

In today's world, virginity is still quite prevalent; we assume that because we're educated, it doesn't matter; nevertheless, the problem is that this perception has nothing to do with education and has everything to do with society. Against Indian society, where being a virgin is a source of pride. In Western society, if you are a virgin, you may be perceived as a loser and weak in your circle.

Virginity has two aspects

- natural
- sociological

It's disgusting to judge someone's character on the basis of virginity because it can be lost for numerous reasons like riding a bike, doing sports, etc. It's illogical to conclude it with adulterous intercourse. But having said that does that mean we should accept the notion of being proud of adulterous intercourse, just like in Western societies. There's one valid concern about virginity and it's not because of illogical fear. It can tell about the historical choices of a person and whether a person is emotionally driven or he or she has a habit of being in a relationship. However, it's a possibility, not an evident probability. If you're seeking a long-term relationship, any sign that the individual is emotionally driven and has a tendency of being in several relationships is a warning flag. While in a marriage, that person may repeat their historical choices. In a similar vein, sociologists Jay Teachman found that adulterous sexual intercourse between future couples did not increase the likelihood of divorce, but adulterous intercourse with others did. A study from the 1980s reported similar findings. In an article published in IFS 2018 by Nicholas H. Wolfinger, I found that the median American woman born in the 1980s has had three lovemaking partners in her lifetime. The median American man has had six partners, but only four if he's a four-year college graduate. In sum, the unexpectedly large number of Americans reporting single-lifetime intimate spouses have the happiest marriages. Past one partner, it doesn't make as much of a difference. The overall contrast isn't huge, but neither is it trivial.

A person's sexual history might affect marital happiness in ways that are also more complex than can be captured with a single variable.

There are numerous reasons to expect sample selection bias to affect the outcomes in the end. People who are promiscuous before marriage may continue to be so, after they marry, resulting in unhappy marriages and divorce. The conclusion that I draw is, we shouldn't celebrate or humiliate biological virginity, it's inhumane to judge someone on that basis. However, a person's historical choices and emotionality related to virginity should not be dismissed as wholly innocuous, as its sociological aspects continue to have an impact on the ultramodern world and institutions such as marriage and family.

Why honour killing is prominent in many Muslim countries?

Now, there are many countries with a Muslim majority who are also suffering from the same problem of honour killing and many people justify the act using Islam. The Napoleonic Code Article 324 is a part of the 1810 penal code which has been copied by many countries, that allowed men to put forward the defence of "crimes of passion", claiming provocation or loss of control, in instances such as if a man finds his wife 'in the act' infidelity. Many Muslim countries incorporated this law in their constitution. We see how in Pakistan, honour killing is so prominent. The Britishers drafted the Indian penal code in 1860 that brought leniency on offenders of honour killings and which eventually perpetuates till today. In 1990, Pakistan introduced its version of 'Islamic' criminal law which allowed for compromise between the parties of a murder case.

People who live in cultures of honour, perceive family as the central institution in their society but in Islam, God is the central Institution. It's shocking how people have allowed their cultural illness to oversize the Islamic teachings. In Arabia, before the arrival of Islam, the Arabs used to bury their daughter alive to restore their honour. They used to consider the birth of a girl child as Dishonouring. But Islam explicitly prohibited this act and honoured females by many rights. Killing a spouse or the spouse's lover is homicide. If there is a case of adultery then they are punished with lashes, not death. And this punishment is only possible if one can bring four virtuous witnesses who have seen the act of intercourse with their eyes, this condition is next to impossible to prove unless it's happening in public. Honour killing is a war against the creator, Allah has naturally given the authority to the parents when a child is young but eventually, after a certain age, Allah takes away the authority of parents which is enough evidence to affirm that their child is qualified enough to take life decisions. The role of parents at a later age is to advise their children, not to force them to obey. I agree there are huge responsibilities laid down by our creator towards our parents, our parents deserve the highest honour in this world. But this privilege is no justification for honour killing in Islam. There is an urgent need for political and religious leaders to actively contribute against this injustice. Muslims must reform the way Quran is taught in the madrasas and homes, we must stress understanding the Quran rather than just reciting once a year like a ritual. This book should be rigorously studied, understood and discussed. Because there is no honour, in the killing.

Your thoughts:

VII

Uniform civil code and Shariah

The first question that should arise in your mind is, why are we even discussing laws which are derived from a 1400-year-old book, which has no relevance in this modern world and new lifestyle. Is there something in this obsolete jurisprudence?

To address this, I found the "First Written Constitution of the World": an important document from the Prophet's time: a study of Dr Muhammad Hamidullah's opinions in the international journal of current advance research.

One of the fascinating aspects of this paper is that the historic document of the state's first written constitution was led by a man who was unable to write himself. Dr Muhammad Hamidullah said that Madinah was the first Muslim state to have a written constitution after reviewing the contents of the first chapter of the Charter. As a result, according to Dr Muhammad Hamidullah, it was the world's first constitution in which the ideals of brotherhood, equality, and freedom of action were written down in order to play a role in the political unit.

You might feel that if there is a difference in interpretations of the Quranic verses by different scholars then why are we following it. We must move towards more modern laws which are better. There are two assumptions made in this statement, first is, modern laws won't have different interpretations as they are not divine rather man-made. Is it the reality? when we look at the different constitutions of the world, As the Indian constitution is an amalgamation of many modern constitutions, that's why it's better to take it as an example. In our Indian constitution we find that all fundamental rights are not absolute, they are subjected to certain restrictions and we can't exercise our rights by selective reading of the constitution, similarly, Islamic laws can't be studied in parts, they need to be analyzed in totality

In India, Only the Supreme Court, not the lower courts, has the authority to interpret the Indian constitution in the final instance. There have been countless instances where the Supreme Court has overturned lower court decisions. But why? Even when it is a man-made constitution rather than a divine revelation, they arrive at different conclusions despite the fact that they are reading the same constitution. This is the point I'm trying to get across: no matter what kind of governing laws exist, whether they are man-made or divine, they all require interpretations based on their soul message. No interpretations can go against the basic principles and what we call basic structure. so the way we give liberty of interpretation to scientific or constitutional text, then it shouldn't be a problem to do the same with the religious scriptures, There can be differences in interpretations. The second assumption is that the modern constitution is better than any divine revelation or ancient laws, so let us see.

The modern constitution is mostly founded on science and logic, and there is a significant overlap between what we deem "good" for us and what science and rationality support. There is no doubt that science can be used to create societal standards, this is called positivism in sociology. Early sociologists tried this positivistic research methodology, soon sociologists realized that we cannot completely rely on the positivistic method to aggressively attain objectivity in the endeavour of making grand theories, the biggest hurdle is we can't treat a human as an insentient sample. Unlike scientific trials, the entire universe is a laboratory in sociology, with each sample having its own distinct will. Later sociologists attempted to bridge the gap between positivism and interpretivism. Many sociologists believe that we have crossed the modern era and have entered a post-modern worldview where objectivity does not exist and that everything is subjective, This idea challenges sociology's core goal to bring reform and minimize instability in society by creating a societal manual of guidelines.

The problem with science is it can't tell you what is moral and what is not. And today's rationale is mostly based on subjective morality. Subjective morality means that morality can change over different times and in different places. There is no objectivity. for example in Indian and Asian societies, incest is not moral, but it is gaining acceptability in Western society, and it is only a matter of time before they no longer find it problematic; scientifically you can't prove incest using contraceptives as wrong. But think by yourself, should we be tolerant of this. if we allow this, the institution of family and marriage would fail, and there would be no difference between animal and human societies. I am not demeaning the animal kingdom's norms. However, there is a significant distinction between animals and humans; a human society without laws is chaos. How dangerous it could be, I can think of a lady named Marina Abramovic, who let strangers do anything they wanted to her body for 6 hours — and the results were terrible. . One man used a razor blade to cut her neck and sucked some of her blood. Her clothes had been torn from her body by the third hour. More than one person seized her and sexually assaulted her. They brought her half-naked through the room, placed her on a table, and put a knife between her knees. While Abramovic refused to call it off, luckily, another person present intervened as the artist's finger was moved near the trigger. Someone placed the stacked weapon in her palm and positioned her arm against her throat at one point, demonstrating how vicious so-called educated individuals can be. Here comes the importance of objectivity and the value system, and limitations of subjectivity, and liberal moral paralysis.

Ban on triple talaq

To begin with, there are numerous types of divorce recognised in Islamic law, including triple talaq. However, we must distinguish between "triple talaq" and "instant triple talaq." If we look at the mechanism used in triple talaq, I believe it is the best manner for a divorce to occur since it allows for significant time for reconciliation and reconsideration of the decision, which is important because divorce affects not only the person but also the children. People feel that Islam promotes the patriarchal way of divorce, in which males can divorce a woman directly but women cannot. There are various schools of thought in Islam. Hanafi, Maliki, Shafi'i, and Hanbali are the four major Sunni madhhabs. Shias include the Twelver, Zaidi, and Ismaili. We have several divorce procedures, but I won't go into detail about them, as they are extensively detailed in multiple sources of jurisprudence. In summary, there are several types of a legal divorce in Islam. The first is what we call Talaq, which is initiated by a man or husband, in which the husband is obligated to pay child support regardless of custody, and the divorced woman is entitled to financial support until the end of her waiting period. The divorce rights given to women are of various types, first, is known as tafriq or faskh. This is when a judge approves a woman's divorce without her husband's consent due to any social, physical, or financial harm he may be causing her. To guarantee her safety, the wife or a blood relative can initiate it on her behalf. The other is khul or khula, which refers to a woman's right to divorce her husband for any legitimate reason. In this case, the wife is required to return the dowry that her husband gave her when they married.

However, instant triple talaq, an anti-Islamic rule that has infiltrated into Muslim society and culture. Neither the Quran nor the Sunnah (action of prophet Mohammed peace be upon him) supports instant triple talaq which is seen in WhatsApp messages, phone calls or through letters, etc. Every constitution or law which is not taken care of can be influenced by patriarchy. Many Islamic laws which were revolutionarily good at that time, had been affected by patriarchal interpretations or applications today. One of the examples is instant triple talaq. Similarly, one more important issue which is very much related to this problem is the concept of Halala. This disgusting practice of formality marriage is also a product of patriarchy and instant triple talaq. In the normal triple talaq, the procedure ends up with the idea that, if both the parties do not come to harmony, then after the three waiting periods are over, they can't marry each other even if they want. It's because marriage isn't a game or a joke, but rather a serious commitment. If a man and a woman are unable to come to an agreement after a consequent long waiting period and repeated discussions, it is preferable to get separated because divorce is an avenue provided by religion. if the relationship doesn't work out, So after the two parties have decided on divorce, they are unable to marry again. In normal circumstances, it is unlikely that someone would consider marrying the same person after going through such a protracted divorce process, Let's pretend they got divorced and married someone else. Then hypothetically, if somehow they again get single (either their spouse died or divorced), they can marry again. And it seems quite reasonable to allow this type of remarriage since if he or she realises the importance of their previous relationship after marrying someone else, they should be permitted to marry again. However, when we substitute triple talaq with instant triple talaq, the difficulty arises, because here divorce can happen for no reason, the waiting period or reconciliation period is no more, which is the most important part of the process of divorce. When a husband divorces his wife by instant triple talaq, it's most likely an impulsive decision taken in the phase of anger (our prophet Mohammed peace be upon him said not take any decision in anger and joy, take decision when you are in a neutral state of mind).

Once the man divorced impulsively (through instant triple talaq) and later realizes the mistake, but the divorce is already done, not from an Islamic point of view but by patriarchal interpretations. So then the qazi or so-called religious judge says that they can't marry again unless they are married to the third person. It is disgusting to even think about this concept. The religion which gives so much importance to modesty, shame, and proper conduct, how can it allow this evil act to happen? This is solely due to the law's patriarchal convenience in replacing triple talaq with instant triple talaq. This is an example of patriarchy and ignorance creeping into Islamic legislation. The problem is not the patriarchal interpretation of the law but, the people of the Muslim community being insentient to bring reform and spread the real and true sense of Islamic laws. The top scholars have already acknowledged these evils and they are trying to educate people, but the political heads are not doing enough to educate the Muslim community. If the Muslim community itself doesn't educate and remove evils from the community, then there will be external interventions to bring justice to the victims who are suffering from these laws. In this case, it's a uniform civil code which is the state intervention to ensure justice to women.

A Uniform Civil Code indicates that all members of society, regardless of faith, will be treated equally under a national civil code that will be applied similarly to all. It addresses topics such as marriage, divorce, child support, inheritance, adoption, and property succession. It is founded on the assumption that in modern culture, there is no link between religion and law

The problem arises when we generalize all Indian Muslims as followers of Hanafi interpretation. Although the majority of our rulings come from Hanafi teaching, but the majority of Muslims are oblivious of this fact, they just believe what the imam in the near masjid tells them. Is Hanafi interpretation equivalent to Quran? The answer is no. We should be given the liberty to choose which school of thought we want to follow. Many of us follow some ruling from one school of thought and the rest from others.

Following a school of thought doesn't come with a package. If one is not convinced of a particular interpretation of rule then he or she can choose another. Choosing other schools of thought is not disbelief rather, any of the schools of thought have much coherence with Quran and sunnah as others. No interpretation goes completely against the soul of Islamic teachings but the dimension of perspective is different.

A uniform civil code's objective is not just to bring uniformity to society, but also to promote scientific temper and justice to all segments of society. Many people believe that a uniform civil code should be unanimously accepted because it is based on modern laws, and hence better than Religious texts. However, modernity is not synonymous with good or right, yes for a large part, we can agree that because of rational thinking and scientific temper, there is a huge overlap between modern laws and what we understand of just or good laws. Our Constitution explicitly says that any law enforcement which will go against the Constitution (imbibed rationale and justice) must be nullified. It means that the idea of bringing a uniform civil code is not to only bring uniformity but to bring justice in an envelope of uniformity. So how should a Muslim perceive this code? As this code is mainly left to be applied in marriage, divorce, and adoption, To say whether a uniform civil code should be applied or not we need to first decide whether the pre-existing law in any community is just and whether their implementation can be made effective or not.

So does that mean uniform civil code must be applied to Muslim personal laws, I would say there are two ways to deal with this issue. The first one is to wait for the consensus or forcefully impose a uniform civil code which might bring violence, opposition, and resistance from the Muslim community, and will destroy the diversity of personal and religious freedom, and would be considered an intervention in their religion. Secondly, by inclusivity, we can involve the people in bringing justice. Considering all the laws which come under Islamic jurisprudence without segregating into madhabs or denominations, we will get different laws for the same issue and, we can allow those laws which are in alignment with our constitution and rational, and also serve the purpose. This way the Muslim community won't feel vulnerable rather it will be easier for the people to accept the laws and internalise.

Do Muslims want shariah law?

You may be wondering why, if Islamic laws are reasonable and fair, so many states claiming to have followed Shariah law are not doing well. Anyone with even a passing knowledge of the situation in the Middle East will recognise, that you will be forced to examine the geopolitics of the region, as you will not be able to find answers to the bloodshed and turmoil of the region in religion. It has become an open secret of destabilisation of the middle east and the interest of the west in that region.

In his incisive essay "From Pol Pot to ISIS: 'Anything That Flies on Everything That Moves,'" journalist John Pilger writes: "ISIS is the progeny of those in Washington and London who collaborated to commit an immense crime against humanity by destroying Iraq as both a state and a society."

If I ignore the geopolitical reasons which are pivotal in law and order then, It might be because of the fact that there is no single book of Shariah, and different interpretations of sources can lead to different outcomes. Secondly, no country has fully implemented Shariah.

Majorly, they pick and choose laws and implement them partially wherever they found it complying with their vision. There is no state that has properly adopted it, and numerous countries have merely applied the penalty portion of the Shariah law, which accounts for a maximum of 5% of the entire shariah. Is it, therefore, a utopia to consider its implementation? The answer is no. There are examples of it being implemented throughout history, such as during the time of the Prophet Mohammed (peace be upon him), and one of them is the rule of the second caliph Umar ibn al-Khattab (634-644 CE). Now some people would say as a Muslim, I insidiously want to replace the Indian constitution with Shariah law. But the reality is, Shariah law is already there in all the constitutions around the world. As the constitution has endured property rights to women, the right to choose a life partner, the concept of consent, divorce, equality before the law, freedom to religious minorities, etc. Most of the values enshrined in our constitution are directly or indirectly coherent to the Quran and teachings of the prophet Muhammad (peace be upon him). it's a part of Shariah law to abide by the law of the land, so a Muslim can't be a good Muslim if he or she doesn't abide by the constitution of the land. , If it's so, then where is the difference.

The difference lies in some of the issues, like the way of providing justice, punishment, economy and governance.

For example, in adultery, there is punishment in Islam for both men and women, but in our Indian constitution, there is no punishment for adultery. Charging or paying Interest is not allowed under shariah and many more. A Muslim is not only morally and legally but also religiously obliged to follow the constitution unless there is anything that stops him or her from practising the faith.

The aim of both the governing entities whether a man-made constitution or divine revelation is to ensure justice to humans. In my opinion, Macro-objective and micro-subjective constitutional values could be an ideal type for governance. If a law satisfies and fulfils the objective of providing justice, then the law should prevail, whether it's from a religious doctrine or modern constitution.

Your thoughts:

VIII
Reaction

We can see how the use of social media and YouTube has expanded dramatically in today's world. Simultaneously, we see a lot of reaction channels gaining popularity at the expense of others' hard work. We always denounce this behaviour, but a large number of people continue to watch these channels. I'm not talking about the morality or legality of reaction channels here; rather, I'm talking about a more serious problem of loneliness and an inferiority complex among us. People have become closer "virtually" as technology has brought them closer together. Nowadays, we can easily and frequently get connected to anybody around the world, however, secluded from the people around us, particularly our family. And no amount of online or virtual connection can make up for the experience of being in the real world. That might be one of the reasons for growing loneliness among youth. I sometimes agree with functionalist theorists who argue that if a social institution exists, it must serve a purpose. The rise in reaction channels indicates that it is of a purpose. We feel more social and connected when we watch a video with others. We expect certain reactions from the viewers, and we are delighted when we see them cheering the same way as we do. Sometimes, especially we Indians, feel proud when a foreigner or a fair-skinned person reacts to Indian content. It could also be the result of an inferiority complex seeking validation from those who are supposedly superior. The truth is that we are still colonised in our minds, as evidenced by our obsession with the English language as a class and our blind acceptance of Western values. This covert sense of a less evolved society has caused people in Western countries to do nothing but react to Indian content in order to garner millions of views. That is not their fault; they are benefiting from a mindset we have fostered that craves validation and a transient sense of pride and confidence in our Indianness. On the one hand, technology has provided us with an isolated bubble in which we can explore anything we want, but on the other hand, we have lost the evening gathering for a TV show that we used to have. We were compelled to watch daily soaps because of our mother, we didn't like it, but at least we used to share the emotions. This might be something that Emile Durkheim talked about as, cohesive force of society. The power that holds us together as a group or family. We have earned this ocean of exploration, with the cost of uncertain loneliness. One of the causes for the substantial increase in the suicide rate and reaction channels, is weakened cohesion. We, humans, are social animals, and we must comprehend the significance of the term "social". The first step is to abandon our search for actual companionship in the virtual world. They may make us feel connected for a brief period of time, but this will not endure. What will last, is the amount of effort we put into the people present in our lives who make us feel alive. Even if we fail, we would be in a better position in understanding people and would experience less regret for not doing enough for our loved ones.

Your thoughts:

IX

A Beard

You may have noticed that when you were in your teens or early twenties and tried to grow a beard, your parents, particularly your mother, would have an issue with it. She'll do everything she can, to persuade us not to grow a beard. But why is that? I tried to find reasons behind this nature. At first glance I thought, no matter how old and big we get, we are always children in our parents' eyes, especially in the eyes of Indian mothers, and that this may be one of the reasons why they desire to see us as children. However, they always make certain comments that I want you to pay attention to, such as, Why have you grown a beard like terrorists, like animals, like babas or why have you grown a beard like Muslims(mullahs) and the last one I heard from one of my friends who is not a Muslim. These remarks are made in both Muslim and non-Muslim households. . And definitely, these statements do not hold positive connotations. It gives us an indication that how we see a beard as evil or Muslim. This is how unknowingly and covertly, we become complicit in the labelling of Muslims as terrorists. Former Supreme Court judge J Chelameswar launched a study on police adequacy and working conditions prepared by the NGO Common Cause and the Lokniti Programme of the Centre for the Study of Developing Societies, According to the 2019 Status of Policing in India Report, one in every two police officers believes that Muslims are "naturally prone" to committing crimes.

As Robert Merton said, the labelling process is often the point of no return in the development of deviance. It can lead to isolation, dismissal, ostracism, and, in extreme cases, prison. It can sometimes turn into a self-fulfilling prophecy.

I agree that an untidy beard is unpleasant, but associating it with Muslims and terrorism is not fair, rather Islamophobic.

On the other hand, in mainstream religions such as Hinduism, we can see Lord Brahma with a beard, which is connected with knowledge, Sadhu Saints, and so on. We may observe famous figures with beards in both orthodox Judaism and traditional Christianity. Growing a beard is one of the primary pillars of Sikhism, and it is also recommended in Islam. But it's disheartening that when we compare our child growing a beard to a terrorist or an animal in a Muslim home, we don't fully consider the ramifications. We sometimes overlook the fact that growing a beard and shortening moustaches is a sunnah (action) of our Prophet Muhammed (peace be upon him). But it's the weakness of our community that we can't hold onto our religious obligations. We can debate whether it is obligatory or not, but there is no doubt whatsoever that facial hair is recommended in the religion.

Maybe I am focusing on a very insignificant dogma, when I see how we have lost the fundamental values of our religion like empathy, honesty, righteousness, etc. Recently, in a case where a senior police officer(Muslim) had to shave, as it is not allowed to grow a beard in the service, but at the same time, Sikhs are allowed in all the services. Here I am not emphasizing whether we should be allowed to keep a beard (like Sikhs) in the army or not, but I am more focused on the reasons why the Supreme Court of India didn't consider a beard an important obligation. It said that "not all Muslims keep a beard" so it can't be considered a fundamental obligation. Even though I can say that Supreme Court shouldn't solely decide what is fundamental to a religion without looking at the scriptures, but at face value, our supreme court is spitting the truth. My focus is on how we, as a community, are more liable for this condition because, we are unconcerned with basic sunnah (action of Prophet peace be upon him). It may not affect everyone, but it does affect those who want to follow it uncompromisingly. The way Sikhs are respected the way they are, we should learn from them how to contribute to society while yet maintaining our faith. The only point to take away from this is that we should not dissuade our children from following the sunnah out of fear or stigma. Or, at the very least, to avoid associating a beard with evil.

Your thoughts:

X

Ban on burqa

It is interesting that eating raw meat, child marriage, superstitions, etc are considered regressive because these things were prevalent in ancient times. Our primitive ancestors used to do these things. The invention of fabric and clothes is considered progress. From roaming naked we progressed by wearing clothes.

Our society evolved from wearing leaves to jeans and t-shirts, we used to call ourselves civilized because we are covered and our ancestors weren't. We look at the tribals as not modern when we see them dancing wearing leaves. But now when we see women wearing hijab or niqab, any traditional dress that covers the body, we directly relate it with oppression and control of sexuality. If we have a broader look into the time scale and definition of being called civilized and empowered, we can see a cycle that goes from dressing less(uncivilized) to dressing more (civilized) and now from dressing more (oppressed) to dressing less(liberated).

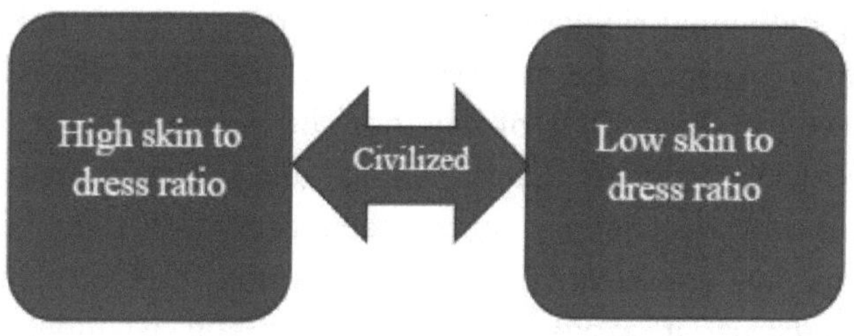

Skin to dress ratio vs civilised

The reversal of moral paradigm and definition of being liberated or empowered is fluid from a liberal perspective.

The west has always defined what is civilized and empowered. Some evolutionary sociologists have defined society as an evolving entity, where European countries are more evolved, this categorization of societies justified colonialism. Non-Europeans were called barbaric and uncivilized.

Eurocentrism is still alive and well around the world. Many revolutionary ideas originated in Europe, contributing to the eradication of societal dysfunctions and dictating how the modern world should look. However, we should not blindly follow a value system just because it has originated in Europe.

First and foremost, Islam teaches modesty to both men and women. The first commandment of Allah is for males to lower their sight and be modest and courteous. The women are then told to cover themselves. Now, the level of modesty varies with culture and country. For example, in India, it is acceptable to display the waist in a saree, but this is not the case in western countries. However, a woman is not coerced to wear only a burka. She has the freedom to choose within the ambit of modesty. If we go by individual rights, then it should be a woman's right to wear anything she chooses (within the public display of decency). Regardless of whether she wears a burqa or a skirt. we criticise Saudi Arabia and North Korea for imposing restrictions on women's dressing, at the same time we appreciate France for banning the burqa and headscarf, it exposes the hypocrisy and Islamophobia inside us. We should try to be consistent with the logic, that we base our decisions on. If forcing someone to wear something is wrong, then restricting that person's to choose is also terrible. If a state shouldn't dictate what to wear, a state should also not dictate what not to wear.

An argument supporting a ban on niqaab could be national security. If national security is the concern, then only niqab can be banned not hijab. There are two extremes: on the one hand, the government wants to outlaw all Islamic dress for national security reasons, while on the other hand, the Muslim community does not want to work together to solve the problem. The Muslim community must understand that this fear among the people is valid to some extent, the way Muslims have been represented in media has ignited the inferno of Islamophobia. So, what is the solution? It is the middle path. Take, for example, security is the concern, because the burqa covers the face, and with globalization, there is growing fear of terrorism. However, due to this pandemic, it has become compulsory to wear a mask everywhere. If you are not Islamophobic, there should be no difference between a mask and a burqa for you. Both items of clothing, in some manner, conceal the identity. The burqa is seen as a symbol of oppression, what if it is a personal choice? If one still believes there is a difference between a mask and a burqa, then sure there is. This is a religious distinction. The only reason you can claim to ban the burqa but not the mask, when you have a preconceived notion that only Muslims can be terrorists and that Muslims have a monopoly on it. However, when we look at the facts and statistics, they are quite contrary. One piece of research on body count by Naveed S. Sheikh, who analysed the death tolls from acts of political violence(war, civil war, democide, and structural violence) of mass killings throughout history. He found that the number of people killed in different civilisations is highest among Christians, anti-theists, Sinics, Buddhists, and primal indigenous peoples, followed by Islamic civilisation, and finally the indic civilisation. One can claim, that this data can be biased by the background of the author. So let us see something from other sources, Cases of white supremacy killings are more than double that of violence by Islamic extremists. But the research found that any act of violence in which the perpetrator is Muslim, receives 758% more major media house coverage in the USA. Disparities in news coverage of assaults based on the perpetrator's religion could explain why people fear "Muslim terrorists" while dismissing other threats. (reference: Erin M. Kearns, Allison E. Betus & Anthony F. Lemieux (2019): Why Do Some Terrorist Attacks Receive More Media Attention Than Others?, Justice Quarterly, DOI: 10.1080/ 07418825.2018.1524507.

So claiming for a ban on Islamic outfits is based on irrational fear. As a society, we have learned and adapted to this abnormal situation. Let's ask ourselves, how often we are requested to reveal our faces and verify our identities on the street. We might have asked for verification while travelling abroad, then, Why is there such a hysterical reaction to the burqa?.

From the example of the mask, it is absolutely conceivable to run a society where women can wear burqa or hijab without the fear of national security. Then where is the problem, the problem is due to growing protectionism policy, Islamophobia, and polarization of vote bank. We as individuals cannot bring about change overnight, but the Muslim community's first move should be to give the state the benefit of the doubt and begin a dialogue on national security without being upset. We should not be upset if a security officer wants to check an individual's identity; they have every right to do so. If we want to enable women to wear burqas, we must also have the maturity to cooperate with the state to eradicate the fear of national security. We can put a condition that only a female officer should be allowed to verify and proceed with the security process. Cooperation is the key to a solution, the only way to deal with contentious issues is to strive for the middle path.

Your thoughts:

XI
Humanity and Religion

Many times people say that we should believe in humanity. Humanity should be our priority and to sound politically correct, we affirm that humanity is what we would choose over religion. The question is posed with the belief that one must choose humanity over religion in order to blame religion for all other ills. It's a risky question because if you appear to be trying to justify religion, you'll be labelled an extremist. This, in my opinion, is a ludicrous question posed by one who believes that religion and humanity are mutually exclusive.

One of my friends asked me the same question and I chose religion. As she know me well, she got annoyed with my selection. Then, I discovered that her idea of religion and humanity was entirely different from mine. This question is faulty in several ways, particularly in academia, because the terms religion and humanity, by their very nature, are ambiguous. When we look into the academic world, we see that no sociologists have ever succeeded in developing a grand theory on religion. It means that numerous ideas attempt to explain religion, but it remains undefined and undefined borders are unknown. When people consider this subject, they may think about one religion rather than the other. When asked to people of different religions, this question becomes subjective. So, if someone were to ask me this question, I would respond by referring to Islam. Even though I don't know much about other religions, because I'm not a student of comparative religion, but I would say any religion consider humanity in one way or other in their ambit. I looked for a proper definition of humanity but couldn't find one. Most sources stated that humanity is defined by humane behaviour, compassion, sympathy, and kindness in general. It is so humancentric, that we associate any good with "human"-ity, not animality or any other way, as if only humans are capable of doing good deeds.

When it comes to religion, Emile Durkheim, a well-known sociologist, defined religion as a "unified system of beliefs and practises relative to sacred things"

So how can they be compared if they have completely distinct definitions?

As all religions are distinct from one another, they will have various perspectives on humanity. Humanity is an aspect of religion, or it can be considered a subset of religion, even though humanity has a broader spectrum of cohesion. Religions are split and have narrowed their sphere of influence to a small number of people, but the unifying force inside religion is much stronger, which could lead to conflict between individuals of different faiths. However, we cannot say that the contrast will definitely become contentious for a variety of reasons, which will be explained below. One can ask " If humanity means kind and sympathetic behaviour towards all humans then how can religion be its superset, despite being divided into many. And generally, people tend to feel that if there was humanity as one religion, we wouldn't be having this many problems and hate. This could be the most beautiful thing that can happen to humankind,

This concept looks impressive at first glance and reminds me of Karl Marx who gave an idea of communism (if we exclude the dictatorship of the proletariat, the dream of an absolutely equal society is enthralling). Although both talks about absolute equality and love, but they are utopian. Humans can't be absolutely unified, there would be disagreements and diversity no matter what. And these differences would lead to struggle, which is happening today. Despite the cohesive nature of many religions, they are not free from the internal tussle. So because of its vague and limited definition of humanity, humanity as religion can't solve human problems, as our problems also include punishment, crime, deterrence, and militarization. Religion sometimes catalyzes acts of humanity eg charities. Charity is not only kindness but a compulsion on every believer of the faiths like Sikhism, Islam etc. In Hinduism, the entire world is regarded as a family. On a similar note, prophet Muhammad(PBUH) said, "One who spends the night with a full stomach while his neighbour is hungry, has not believed in me. One who spends the night clothed, while his neighbour has no clothes, has not believed in me."

However, sometimes people manipulate the teachings of religion for their dominance and greed. Most of the time, we unconsciously associate every good deed with humanity and every bad deed with religion; if a person does good, we generally comment " its humanity", but we don't bother to consider whether the act was inspired by religion or not, we forget to acknowledge that his or her act of kindness may have been inspired by religion, no doubt we can categorize it as humanity, but not only under the ambit of humanity, as religion inspires and drive humans towards good. Without the conception of hell and heaven, or fear of state and law, humanity would be merely a choice or utopia, religion or state gives humanity a more rigid understanding, that if we fail to oblige or perform, we would be held accountable.

If we remove religion from this picture, nobody can endorse humanity. As assisting a blind person crossing the road is a universally accepted good, if I am late for work and see a blind person attempting to cross the road, it is not obligatory for me to assist him, and capitalism and individualism may justify this act so well that no one can challenge it. What if an oppressive regime is persecuting a group of people? Don't you think our fear would overshadow our desire to resist? Why should our society's financial elite pay taxes? Because the government has mandated it, and every time they uncover a loophole, they try to find ways to go across it. Although there are cases where humanity can drive someone to do all of the above deeds. if I believe in the Day of Judgment, I'd be more conscious of my actions and compelled to take action. Yes, religion sometimes prescribes or proscribe actions that do not appear to be humanitarian, but that is always a subject of discussion. For example, while humanity may prohibit the death penalty, certain religions and governments tolerate it for the sake of larger human good by removing individuals who commit heinous crimes (heinous crimes are again subjective for different religions). I've not discussed out how religion may mobilise individuals to commit something inhumane since, we're all aware of that;

the focus of the article was to show the other side of the coin, and how religion is essential to humanity's survival. If we had relied on mere humanity instead of "dharma" to judge the Mahabharata, it would be impossible to determine who should have won the fight. Pandavas' unbridled gambling, Draupadi's propertization on the one hand, and Kauravas' ambition and greed to seize whatever the Pandavas had on the other. We would not be learning different lessons from this legend if it weren't for Lord Krishna's reinforcement of a woman's modesty and what is right, above all other wrongdoings. For the time being, I have not studied other religions, but I believe that any religion's basics teach the same thing. Even though I am not a scholar, I analysed this subject from an Islamic standpoint, and everything I have studied thus far barely goes against humanity or the improvement of society. To be a religious or a follower of any faith, the first requirement is to be a human being. I've discovered that some religious tenets are far superior to the basic premise of humanity. In Hinduism, for example, the entire world is regarded as a family or one body. The duty and responsibilities of a person towards his or her parents, neighbours, sick people, the elderly, minorities, animals, plants, women, and children are all expressly mentioned in religion. Even in combat, a Muslim is not authorised to physically or mentally harm an innocent person. We are not permitted to slander somebody, which is a very easy thing to do these days. During my undergraduate years, whenever we saw a girl and a boy together, we assumed they were dating without hesitation. It was simply unconcerned. That was something that everyone did, including myself. We used to term a girl with numerous boys "characterless" and a boy as "playboy". It's simple for us and everyone else to make judgments about someone's character. However, after I began reading Islam, I saw how filthy it was. It was slander, which is a serious sin. Even if a boy and girl are dating, a Muslim is not allowed to comment on their interaction (hence the idea of providing four pious witnesses who must have witnessed them performing the act of intimacy comes; however, it is practically impossible to provide four pious witnesses watching that act until it is not in a public place; this was done to ensure public display of decency).

We are supposed to have a positive and non-slanderous way of judging people. We are permitted to denounce the act of violation, but not to identify somebody as wicked, because there is always the possibility of repentance.

When it comes to spreading slander, a Muslim's default position is to offer the benefit of the doubt. There are numerous instances in which I encountered a tremendous level of generosity in religion that goes beyond today's sense of humanity. Many people are engaged in humanitarian activities and labour selflessly. There may come a time in one's life when they believe they are doing enough, and there is nothing wrong with that from a humanitarian standpoint, but religion keeps us on our toes. In the name of constant philanthropy, we cannot be lenient. ". Sometimes we justify some act which is done in a state of frenzy by saying that " It wasn't me, it's my anger " or " I didn't mean it " or " It's because of adrenaline, it's biology, not me". In religion, we are usually held responsible for our acts rather than our ideas, yet there is always a transitional period during which we may control our thoughts by allowing certain thoughts to settle and others to just pass through our minds. If you're still sceptical, consider this: according to some neuroscientists, we have 60,000 to 80,000 thoughts per day, but how many do you remember precisely? We recall what we wish to remember or what has a strong enough influence on our cellular consciousness to be remembered. In the Quran, Allah declares that we will be interrogated about what we heard, what we saw, and about our hearts. This means if you have said or done something wrong (abused, humiliated, shamed, etc) in that state of emotion, you may not be held accountable by law by blaming it on hormones or you may get forgiveness from the victim, but you will be asked for this action in the hereafter.

There are some people who associate many ills in our society directly with religion. Like al Qaeda and ISIS used religion to mobilize the masses for their political motive, but we can't ignore that western forces have contributed enough to destabilize and control the oil-rich region. American leaders have admitted that they were behind the formation of these militant organisations, which were originally formed to oppose the Soviet Union. Most unstable states have one thing in common, that's oil. Coincidentally, they have the majority's religion as Islam. Is Islam the cause of the chaos? If so, why are countries like Indonesia, Bangladesh, Pakistan, the United Arab Emirates, Saudi Arabia, Azerbaijan, Turkey, and others not in the middle of a war? The line that separates Saudi Arabia from the rest of the Middle Eastern countries, is its intimate relationship with America. Those who did not comply with America, such as Libya, Iran, and Iraq, are either in a war zone or in the midst of a civil war. As a result, anyone who has done even a little research and understands the geopolitics of the Middle East would never blame the mess on religion. Kashmir has long been a source of contention between India and Pakistan. if we do otherisation of this issue, one can say it's Hindu vs Muslims, but as an Indian, we know why there is so much resentment between these two countries, it's because of historical and political reasons, not religious ones. Nowadays, mob lynching has become a social fact or a new normal in our country just like rape, murder, etc. but does that mean we have to blame Hinduism for this. I have not seen anything in the religion which can lead to this act. The common puzzle between a mob lynching and an exodus of Kashmiri pundits is the dominance of the majority over the minority. These people have one thing in common, they are the most uninformed people of the religion, who think they are doing for the religion, but instead making a mockery of their belief. These people don't need religion to assert their dominance, even if you remove religion from the context, they would have done the same thing using caste, gender, ethnicity, race, etc. Religion is one of the tools in their toolset. Yes, there are several cultural and religious customs that can bring inhumane practices and can go against today's conceived morality standards.

The point here is not to glorify religion over humanity but to acknowledge that these two are incomparable social quantities or social facts. It's just like comparing propellers with an aeroplane.

So next time you encounter this debate, try to avoid hyper simplification and start to think rationally. No matter what you choose but now you know, their existence is not a duality.

"Humanity without religion is toothless and religion without humanity is chaos".

Your thoughts:

XII

Hurdle in democracy

Democracy has always been a target for many. But I would like to draw your attention to Bollywood movies. You must have encountered some of the events in any movie where we see the whole setup of the judiciary, and the framed innocent or hero of the story couldn't get justice out of the judiciary. We get emotional and so does the audience attending the prosecution. We can tell which film depicts an anti-democratic notion and which does not. At that time I used to wonder why the court doesn't listen to the general public and give judgment in favour of the character playing hero.

But now I understand why they couldn't do that. It's because what the majority feels to be true can't necessarily be true. In the context of our country, we are moving towards majoritarianism. It is not a sign of healthy democracy when a lawyer bases his or her argument on emotions rather than facts and receives a favourable verdict. It is also true that our judicial system is overburdened with cases; many cases in which the perpetrator is released on bail due to a lack of evidence. The failure of investigating agencies, corrupt officials, and outdated technologies are all contributing factors. As a result, it is the judiciary's responsibility to keep the constitution at the forefront and not be swayed by majority sentiment.

Socrates, a great thinker, despised democracy because he believed that it would inevitably lead to populist control. He used the analogy of a confectioner and a doctor, arguing that in a democracy, people would vote for the confectioner rather than the doctor, especially when the masses are uneducated. Voting is a democratic skill, not a birthright. Majoritarianism is becoming more prevalent in India and around the world. Persecution and exodus of Kashmiri pundits, mob lynching, minorities in Pakistan, Uighurs in China, Rohingyas in Myanmar, and so on are only a few examples.

We are witnessing a shift in global politics towards religion and protectionism at this moment. This is a huge stumbling block, particularly in developing countries.

In our schools, colleges, and day-to-day encounters, we have been avoiding religious education. We anticipated that as the governing system became more secular, religions would become less active and withdraw from the social and cultural realms, but the fact is that religions have discovered methods to seep into modern society, or, to put it another way, religion has never retreated from society. Religion is making a comeback in many nations, including Russia, Hungary, Peru, Venezuela, India, and Turkey, as a result of a right-wing political shift. In politics, there is a sinusoidal cycle of left and right, and all ideologies have an equal probability of reaching extremes, but the danger is that democratic institutions and democratic norms are corroded.

When educated individuals of society refuse to discuss an issue, it will remain controversial. Discourses and dialects can help to resolve the majority of conflicts. Instead of running away from religion, our approach should be inclined towards creating a safe campus environment for discourses. Most of the acts of violence and oppression in the name of religion have a broad base of uneducated and misinformed people mobilized for political motives. The more educated they would be about their faith the more they could develop an intellectual conscience to judge right and wrong.

"*The best way to deal with religion is to deal with it*".

Your thoughts:

Criticism

- There are many instances where you can't simply compare based on science. No doubt, that anybody can feel uncomfortable irrespective of the gender. when a girl being stared by a stranger in an inappropriate manner and at the same time when this happens with a boy , the level of uncomfortableness is different. Yeah, we can't clearly say the exact level but saying like concept of level of uncomfortable is vague and we should follow equal criminalisation for any genders, if we consider that act as an offence or a crime in case of a girl, we can go for that but we can never equalise uncomfortableness of a girl being a victim and a boy being a victim. Staring a girl simple on her face is way different than staring throughout her body as it raises a question over her modesty. *(Sayed Nishat Tanaum)*

Response:

It has nothing to do with men or women, study shows that disturbing stares are always compelling because they offer the starer the power to make you feel victimised, no matter what the intention is. Studies have demonstrated that starring has an impact on people's behaviour regardless of gender. The consequences are more noticeable in people with disabilities, people of different skin colours, and so on. Our brain interprets staring as a hint that you're different or out of the ordinary. This might boost one's confidence, but it can also have a negative impact. However, once you notice and perceive a stare, you become conscious of yourself. The starer starts feeling that they have an undue right to judge you, to make you feel uncomfortable. This is something you don't yield to them, but they still take from you by force.

I agree that the level of discomfort experienced by men and women differs. However, this does not rule out the possibility of a man experiencing discomfort. The point of this article is to highlight why is it different? Are men biologically programmed to be less bothered by stares? I don't see any supporting evidence, so there must be some societal influence on our behaviour. The fundamental reason for this could be that modesty is primarily associated with women, and it is a two-edged sword. It is harmful to both genders because it allows society to place a high value on women's modesty over men's. This basically translates as, only a woman's modesty can be offended, hence society must be more restrictive toward women in order to ensure their purity. Secondly, it numbs society towards the violation of the modesty of men. This is one of the reasons we still find it difficult to accept that men can also be harassed. This mentality has not only hyper regulated women but has considered men as invincibly modest.

- You are defending the traditional institutions, Are you a conservative? (Shubhangi Sahay)

Response:

Even if I observe clear proof of ideological affiliation, I refrain from labelling someone. Labelling of a person seizes the avenue for reform and change, even if they want to. As a result, I won't refer to myself as a conservative or a liberal. In general, liberals refer to me as a conservative, and conservatives refer to me as a liberal. So this claim does not surprise me. But, for the sake of argument, even if I have defended some of the traditional Institutions. The question is, is it wrong? Defending some of the traditional institutions like marriage, family, etc, which are more functional than some modern institutions, is not wrong. I have used the scientific method, rationale, induction and deduction to reach organic conclusions. The question has a preconceived belief in synonymity of modernity and liberalism with good, right and correct. Neither conservativism nor liberalism can do this dangerous claim of their synonymity with absolute truth, right and good.

- Your choice of content has a lopsided Islam favouring tone? (Sayed Nishat Tanaum)

Response:

I won't say I have favoured one religion over others, as I have not done any comparative analysis among religions. Yes, this book contains a significant portion about Islam, I also felt it while writing. But I had limitations of lack of knowledge and understanding about other religions and faiths. As a born Muslim, I know Islam more than any other religion. The Islamic perspective is an effort to make the readers aware of their understanding of religion and introspect about the actions in their life.

- Your idea has generally targeted women and seems to be misogynistic?(Shubhangi Sahay)

Response:

The fact that a man is writing about women is ironic in and of itself. However, articles and manuscripts produced by both male and female researchers were found in my deductive observations. So, I'm not alone in writing about these issues; a diverse group of people from both genders have been part of these studies, and they've attempted to highlight some of the issues that disproportionately affect or involve women, but I have tried my best to include both genders equally responsible and aware of their role. There is nothing in this book or in my mind that opposes women's empowerment, but my goal is to highlight that women's empowerment does not always imply men's disempowerment. Both genders should work together for the greater good by ensuring equality of justice.

LAST WORDS

Some readers may have found some of the content offensive, and while I tried to adopt a multidimensional approach and do justice to the rationale, several subject matters required a linear approach due to the abundance of lopsided information available.

In the pursuit of finding the truth, we must risk being offensive to some extent, being offended doesn't make you right or wrong, it means your intellect and conscience are alive, you are alive. The best way to deal with any contention is Moderation.

In Quran, it says "Oh people of the book, don't go extreme in religion"(Surah An-Nisa:171)

In Michael Hart's book THE 100, the man who is voted #1 in the race of history's most influential person, Prophet Muhammad, said," Beware of extremism in religion, for it destroyed those before you"

In Aristotle's doctrine, " virtue exists as a mean state between the vicious extremes of excess and deficiency.

So, the best way is the middle path in all the spheres of our life. Our Education system is impotent to cultivate critical thinking in the minds of people.

"The art of critical thinking, to rationally acknowledge the reality of multiple truths by accepting differences, is as important as the existence of humankind".

9 798885 461511

Printed by Libri Plureos GmbH in Hamburg,
Germany